A Pocket Guide to the U.S. Constitution

A Pocket Guide to the U.S. Constitution

I confess that there are several parts of this constitution which I do not at present approve, but I am not sure I shall never approve them…

Thus I consent, Sir, to this Constitution because I expect no better, and because I am not sure, that it is not the best. The opinions I have of its errors, I sacrifice to the public good…

On the whole, Sir, I can not help expressing a wish that every member of the Convention who may still have objections to it, would with me, on this occasion doubt a little of his own infallibility, and to make manifest our unanimity, put his name to this instrument.

Benjamin Franklin, September 17, 1787
(Last day of the Constitutional Convention)

A Pocket Guide to the U.S. Constitution

Commentary by
Andrew B. Arnold, Ph.D.
History Department
Kutztown University of Pennsylvania

Learning Solutions

New York   Boston   San Francisco
London   Toronto   Sydney   Tokyo   Singapore   Madrid
Mexico City   Munich   Paris   Cape Town   Hong Kong   Montreal

Pearson Learning Solutions, 501 Boylston Street, Suite 900, Boston, MA 02116
A Pearson Education Company
www.pearsoned.com

Printed in the United States of America

1 2 3 4 5 6 7 8 9 10 V3DZ 15 14 13 12 11 10

000200010270650294

SB

ISBN 10: 0-558-87444-4
ISBN 13: 978-0-558-87444-5

Purpose

This book tells you what experts assume you already know.

The available pocket-sized and back-of-the-textbook Constitutions don't do enough. They format the Constitution like a short story. They leave out the names of articles, sections, and clauses. They leave out the standard numbering system. They don't define basic terms.

My students need this information, so familiar to lawyers and scholars. When I ask students to turn to the "Commerce Clause," I want us to end up in the same place (Article 1, Section 8, Clause 3). And when we get there, I want them to know what it means.

Most non-pocket guides have the opposite problem. They tend to be massive and impenetrable. Scholars and lawyers examine the Constitution case by case, topic by topic, amendment by amendment. They use a specialized language. They assume their readers already know the subject, as well as the legal and scholarly debates.

But the Constitution is not only a matter of scholarly, legal debate; it is part of the way Americans live. It is how we understand our rights and obligations as people and as A People—every day. We need a guide that will fit in a pocket, briefcase, or backpack. We need a way to answer basic questions that arise day to day, or in a class period, or in the course of reading more in-depth books on the topic.

This book is a place to begin to understand the United States Constitution. It is as complete as I can make it and still have it fit in your pocket. It's as simple as I can make and still have it be accurate.

Andrew B. Arnold, Ph.D.
Kutztown, Pennsylvania

Note to the Reader

The text in gray boxes is the actual text from the Constitution. The text following each gray box explains that section of the Constitution.

The headings on each page will orient you as to where you are in the Constitution. Constitutional clauses are numbered in three parts, according to their Article, Section, and Clause. Thus, for example, the Apportionment (Three Fifths) Clause is numbered 1.2.3. That is:

Article 1	Legislative
Section 2	House of Representatives
Clause 3	Apportionment (Three Fifths) Clause

Brief Contents

Detailed Contents

Constitution and Amendments

I. Structure and Preamble
"We the people . . ."

The basic structure of the Constitution is straightforward. First, it lays out the powers of the legislature, executive, and judiciary. ①
Second, it creates a means for enacting itself as supreme law. Third, ②
it creates a way to amend itself. In addition to these basic tasks, ③
its Preamble sets out larger goals in the name of the People, and another section limits state sovereignty.

The first Congress added a set of 10 amendments known as the Bill of Rights – rights held by the People against the national government. We have added another 17 amendments since then. All are part of the Constitution.

The core structure of the Constitution then:
    I. Preamble (statement of purpose)
    II. Three Branches of Government (Legislative, Executive, Judicial)
    III. Limitations on State Sovereignty
    IV. Ratification, Amending, and National Supremacy
    V. Bill of Rights and other Amendments

The Framers wrote the Constitution with one eye always on ratification. They avoided overly precise language in areas such as slavery and limits of state and federal sovereignty.

The Constitution's complexity comes from interaction of all its moving parts, its deliberate vagueness, and the battles won and lost on its meaning. Legislative, Executive, Judiciary, and People insist that *their* privileges ought to be paramount. The artful efforts of the Framers to evade certain issues (slavery, judicial power. . .) left plenty of room for interpretation.

Yet the accepted need for Constitutional stability has meant that once a branch in one generation won a battle over its interpretation, it has tended to stick. For a time, anyway.

Preamble

We the People of the United States, in Order to form a more perfect Union, establish Justice, insure domestic Tranquility, provide for the common defence, promote the general Welfare, and secure the Blessings of Liberty to ourselves and our Posterity, do ordain and establish this Constitution for the United States of America.

Function of Preamble

This introduction to the Constitution served as a ringing opening and a rhetorical link to the Declaration of Independence. It reminded readers of the republican and liberal ideals of the Revolution. It reminded people at that time of the new government's ultimate goals. It reminds us today that salesmanship was much on the minds of the authors. They feared for its ratification. The Committee of Detail, assigned the task of creating a final document added this as a finishing touch.

Defining Liberal and Republican

The terms have mutated, though historians and political scientists often use them in their original sense, or try to. The term "liberal" referred to sacred individual liberties (life, liberty, and property). In Social Contract political theory, individuals retained such rights under a just government. Such theory was at the heart of Western European and American political theory. The term "republican" referred to an ideology of the American Revolution that relied on citizens to put the public good ahead of private interests.

"We the People of the United States"

An earlier draft originally named the thirteen states instead of "United States." But the Committee of Detail changed this since the Constitution declared itself to be ratified once a mere 9 of the 13 states approved it. Any states that failed to do so would be outside the new nation. By so ratifying these *united states* continued the historical process of creating a *nation* called the "United States."

"People"

This was the "people" of individual states, united in federation, not the people of the United States. Somewhat. The Declaration of Independence had already described Americans as a "people." Observers such as John Adams and Patrick Henry referred to both their state *and* the United States as their "country." Over time increasingly, Americans came to see themselves as a single, diverse people, simultaneously members of their town, state, and nation (also ethnicity, party, religion, and sports team fanbase. The Constitution does not endorse a team.)

"form a more perfect Union"

This phrase suggests a wish to differentiate the Constitution from the then-governing Articles of Confederation. Since the Articles established a "perpetual union" this phrase became a way for pro-Union analysts during the Civil War to insist that the union of the Constitution must also be perpetual.

"establish Justice. . . and our Posterity"

These phrases name the goals that the Constitution is attempting to achieve. The terms "common defence" and "general welfare" appear in section 8 of the Articles. The Convention named these goals in the first resolutions that it adopted on May 29, 1787 (The Committee of Detail added "liberty.") On May 30, they decided that to achieve these goals would require wholesale changes to the Articles.

"do ordain and establish"

This claim, combined with the ratification process described the Constitution as basic law. This placed it above national and state legislatures, as well as the previous Articles. The new government would rule by virtue of a sovereignty new to political philosophy: "the people." (Not god, custom, military victory or personal authority.)

II. Three Branches of Government

1. Legislative (Congress)
2. Executive (President)
3. Judicial (Courts)

The first three articles laid out conflicting powers and responsibilities of the three branches. This underlines a main point of the Constitution: It created a government that would, in its very structure, check and balance the ability of any one part to become tyrannical. These branches battle for power and function. They also jockey for position with the people, states, political parties, and private powers.

But the roles of the branches have been defined in practice as much as in the text of the Constitution. The Court spent its first decade establishing its role as the arbiter of the Constitution's meaning. The House became more of a collection of local voices. The Senate, originally assumed to represent the states, became more of a national voice. Executive powers expanded most greatly during wars, and with New Deal federal agencies under Franklin D. Roosevelt.

Laws must be passed separately in the Senate and House of Representatives. The houses then confer to negotiate any differences between their respective versions. The President can choose to sign or veto. Bureaucrats in the Executive Branch can enforce with gusto or indifference. The Court can invalidate. People and states resist or not.

All parties have come to know this set of Constitutional and practical limitations in advance. In the normal course of events, gaining the approval of all parties has become part of negotiations from the beginning. Bills are developed in full awareness of the legal context created by the Court's previous decisions. Public Representatives in House, Senate, Executive and states weigh in, as do private lobbyists and individuals.

Article 1 Legislative (Congress)
Section 1 Legislative Power Defined

> **Clause 1.1 Legislative Power Defined**
> All legislative Powers herein granted shall be vested in a Congress of the United States, which shall consist of a Senate and House of Representatives.

The First Branch of Government

The founders saw the legislature as the leading branch of government. It was, after all, the most directly responsible to the people, and to the states.

"All legislative Powers...vested" (Delegation Doctrine)

The Constitution vested (gave) "all" legislative power to Congress. For this reason, the Court rejected the 1933 National Industrial Recovery Act (It ceded power to define "fair" codes without enough Congressional oversight or definition of terms. *Schechter Poultry Corp. v. US* (1935)).

Senate and House of Representatives

The split, "bicameral" legislature was a standard feature in most state constitutions. The lower house was intended to be more democratic, and the upper house to be more insulated from democracy.

Great Compromise

The split, or "bicameral" legislature helped settle a conflict over the basis of representation. During the Convention, delegates from smaller states insisted that legislative power be equally divided among every state. More populous states insisted that power be set by population levels. They compromised. They agreed to base the lower house on population, thus giving larger states greater representation in that body. The smaller states would have equal representation in the Senate, however.

8

Section 2 House of Representatives

> **Clause 2.1 Composition of House**
> The House of Representatives shall be composed of
> Members chosen every second Year by the People of the
> several States, and the Electors in each State shall have the
> Qualifications requisite for Electors of the most numerous
> Branch of the State Legislature.

"the Electors in each State shall have the"

This is one of the rare places where the Constitution defines the
right to vote. Although it leaves the specifics to the states, Section
1.4.1 below gives Congress the right to make laws concerning
those specifics.

"by the People"

The Court has used this term to judge the fairness of voting districts. State districts should be equal in population so each person's
vote is worth the same (*Wesberry v. Sanders* (1964)). The Court
largely sees "Gerrymandering" (shaping districts to give one party
or candidate a demographic advantage) to be a political issue. See
14th Amendment "Equal Protection and The Vote" below.

> **Clause 2.2 Qualifications for Representatives**
> No Person shall be a Representative who shall not have
> attained to the Age of twenty five Years, and been seven Years
> a Citizen of the United States, and who shall not, when elected,
> be an Inhabitant of that State in which he shall be chosen.

A Representative must 25 years old, an inhabitant of the state in
which he or she is running, and a citizen of the US as of election
day. The Court ruled that states may not create additional qualifications for office, such as term limits (*US v. Thornton* (1995)).

Section 2 House of Representatives, Cont'd

Clause 2.3 Apportionment (Three Fifths Clause)
Apportionment of Taxes and Representatives

Representatives and direct Taxes shall be apportioned among the several States which may be included within this Union, according to their respective Numbers, which shall be determined by adding to the whole Number of free Persons, including those bound to Service for a Term of Years, and excluding Indians not taxed, three fifths of all other Persons. The actual Enumeration shall be made within three Years after the first Meeting of the Congress of the United States, and within every subsequent Term of ten Years, in such Manner as they shall by Law direct. The number of Representatives shall not exceed one for every thirty Thousand, but each State shall have at Least one Representative; and until such enumeration shall be made, the State of New Hampshire shall be entitled to chuse three, Massachusetts eight, Rhode Island and Providence Plantations one, Connecticut five, New York six, New Jersey four, Pennsylvania eight, Delaware one, Maryland six, Virginia ten, North Carolina five, South Carolina five, and Georgia three.

"Representatives and direct Taxes shall be apportioned"'

More populous states were entitled to more votes in the House, and to more Presidential electors. They also paid a higher share of taxes. (The Framers considered—and rejected—wealth as a way to apportion political power.)

"direct taxes"

This provision was intended to spread the taxation burden equally among the people of the states. Note the early focus on treating states equally under the nation. The 16th Amendment finally severed apportionment of taxes from electoral power by permitting Congress to levy income taxes regardless of the census. See 1.9.4 below.

Section 2 House of Representatives, Cont'd

"three fifths of all other Persons" (Three fifths Clause)

The term "other Persons" in this case refers to slaves. Slaves were to be counted as three-fifths of a person when apportioning Representatives, Presidential Electors, or the share of federal taxes among states.

Origins of the "Three-fifths" Ratio

This ratio was a split-the-difference compromise that pleased neither side. (It originated in a failed amendment to the Articles of Confederation in 1783.)

References to Slavery in the Constitution

The term "slavery" does not appear in the Constitution.

3/5 of "other persons" (1.2.3), "such persons" (1.9.1), "No Person held to Service or Labour" (4.2.3). See also the prohibition on a Capitation Tax unless in proportion to Apportionment of Taxes and Representatives (1.9.4). See also last part of Article 5 that forbade any amendments to the articles that guaranteed slaveholder rights.

"Indians not taxed"

It treated Native Americans not quite as citizens, and not quite as sovereign nations. They were not taxed, nor counted for apportionment of House or Presidential Electors. (See 1.8.3 Commerce Clause) See 14th Amendment, Clause 2. Indians gained nominal citizenship in 1924, but states controlled right to vote.

"Term of ten Years"

A national census must be held every ten years in order to accurately apportion Representatives and Presidential electors among the states as population shifts. This clause underlines the importance of a system of representation based on individuals as well as states. State legislatures are responsible for drawing Congressional districts.

Section 2 House of Representatives, Cont'd

"not to exceed one for every thirty Thousand"

It sets a maximum level of representation. *No more* than one for
every 30,000 citizens. The House has never been in danger of
violating this rule. Take the current population of the US, over 300
million. Divide by 30,000, and you would get a House of 10,000
members! Congressional districts now average roughly 700,000
citizens. The House grew until 1911 when it limited itself by law
to 435 members, to be apportioned among all states, including any
new states.

Clause 2.4. Vacancies

When vacancies happen in the Representation from any
State, the Executive Authority thereof shall issue Writs of
Election to fill such Vacancies.

House Vacancies

House vacancies are filled by election, not appointment. If the
vacancy happens early in the two-year term, a special election is
generally held. If late in the term, states generally wait until the
next regular election day. Specific rules differ from state to state.

Clause 2.5 Rules and Impeachment

The House of Representatives shall chuse their Speaker
and other Officers; and shall have the sole Power of
Impeachment

"Speaker and other Officers"

The Speaker sets the agenda of the House. She or he succeeds to
the presidency if the President and Vice President are incapacitated,
and presides over joint sessions except when counting electoral
votes (See the 12th and 25th Amendments.).

Section 2 House of Representatives, Cont'd

"Impeachment"

The House first passes articles of impeachment, acting as a grand jury to decide if a trial is warranted. The Senate trial is based on those articles. See clause 1.3.6 for procedures. Clause 2.2.1a prohibits the President from pardoning impeached officers. Section 2.4 defines who and for what reasons a federal official may be impeached.

Rules

This clause gives the House of Representatives the right to organize itself and set its own rules.

Section 3 Senate

Clause 3.1 Definition of the Senate

The Senate of the United States shall be composed of two Senators from each State, chosen by the Legislature thereof, for six Years; and each Senator shall have one Vote.

"two Senators from each State"

This clause recognizes the sovereignty of the states. Every state, no matter its population, size, or wealth, has the same level of political representation in the Senate.

"chosen by the Legislature thereof"

The original decision to elect Senators by state legislatures reflects the Great Compromise that saw the Senate not only as the upper house, but as representing the states.

Popular Election of Senators

The 17th Amendment, passed in 1913, changed this clause to election by popular vote of each state.

Clause 3.2 Staggering Terms of Office

Immediately after they shall be assembled in Consequence of the first Election, they shall be divided as equally as may be into three Classes. The Seats of the Senators of the first Class shall be vacated at the Expiration of the second Year, of the second Class at the Expiration of the fourth Year, and of the third Class at the Expiration of the sixth Year, so that one third may be chosen every second Year; and if Vacancies happen by Resignation, or otherwise, during the Recess of the Legislature of any State, the Executive thereof may make temporary Appointments until the next Meeting of the Legislature, which shall then fill such Vacancies.

Section 3 Senate, Cont'd

Perpetual Senate; Rules of Procedure

Unlike the House, where every member must be reelected every two years, only 1/3 of Senators run for reelection at a time. Therefore, Senate rules remain in force, while the House approves new rules for each new Congress. This is one reason why traditions and rules such as "holds," "courtesy," and "filibusters" that allow a minority of Senators to prevent action have become such a dense tangle.

Cloture and Filibuster

In 1917 the Senate enacted a "cloture" rule to create a way to end debate. Originally invented to limit filibusters, it became a way to enable them. A Senator can require a vote for "cloture" in order to begin the final vote on a bill. From 1917-1975, cloture required 2/3 of the Senators present. A 1975 rule change required 3/5 of *all* Senators (60 of 100). Cloture to change Senate rules still requires the old standard of 2/3 vote.

"and if Vacancies happen by Resignation, or otherwise"

The 17th Amendment, passed in 1913 and allowing for popular election of Senators, allowed states to provide for special election if they desired.

> ### Clause 3.3 Qualifications for Senators
> No Person shall be a Senator who shall not have attained to the Age of thirty Years, and been nine Years a Citizen of the United States, and who shall not, when elected, be an Inhabitant of that State for which he shall be chosen.

Qualifications for Senators

A Senator must be 30 years old, a US citizen for 9 years, and an inhabitant of the state by *election day*. (Before becoming VP, Joe Biden was elected Senator at age 29, but reached 30 by the time he was sworn in.)

Section 3 Senate, Cont'd

> **Clause 3.4 Role of the Vice President**
> The Vice President of the United States shall be President of the Senate, but shall have no Vote, unless they be equally divided.

"President of the Senate...unless they be equally divided"

When the Senate is tied the VP casts the deciding vote. Outside of this clause, the Vice Presidency remains largely undefined. See also 1.3.5 and impeachment.

Historical Development of Vice Presidency

George Washington saw first VP John Adams as a member of the Legislature; the Senate saw him as a member of the Executive. He thus had little to do. When Adams became President in 1796, his former opponent, Thomas Jefferson used his time as VP to attack him. The 12th Amendment and the political parties tied President and VP together.

Modern Vice Presidency

Recently, VPs have taken on a larger role, depending on agreements between President and VP. They have often become more of an "Assistant President." Starting with Walter "Fritz" Mondale in 1976, VPs have gained offices and staff, and Executive Branch functions.

> **Clause 3.5 Senate Officers**
> The Senate shall chuse their other Officers, and also a President pro tempore, in the Absence of the Vice President, or when he shall exercise the Office of President of the United States.

Senate President Pro Tempore

By law, third in line of succession in case President, Vice President, and Speaker of the House are incapacitated.

Section 3 Senate, Cont'd

Tradition places the senior member of the majority party in this position. It is largely ceremonial. ↳ pres. pro temp

Presiding Over the Senate

In theory, the President Pro Tempore presides over the Senate. In practice, junior Senators fill this job during routine business. This gives them the chance to learn the complex rules of the Senate and parliamentary procedure.

> **Clause 3.6 Senate Impeachment Power**
>
> The Senate shall have the sole Power to try all Impeachments. When sitting for that Purpose, they shall be on Oath or Affirmation. When the President of the United States is tried, the Chief Justice shall preside: And no Person shall be convicted without the Concurrence of two thirds of the Members present.

Senate Impeachment as Trial

Think of a Senate impeachment as a trial. Although the whiff of politics has always been part of such trials, the Senate has consistently stopped short of allowing impeachments to take the place of elections.

> **Clause 3.7 Limits to Impeachment Power**
>
> Judgment in Cases of Impeachment shall not extend further than to removal from Office, and disqualification to hold and enjoy any Office of honor, Trust or Profit under the United States: but the Party convicted shall nevertheless be liable and subject to Indictment, Trial, Judgment and Punishment, according to Law.

Section 3 Senate, Cont'd

"When the President. . . the Chief Justice shall preside"

Obviously, in this case, the Vice President stands to gain the Presidency if the current occupant is impeached. Therefore, he can't preside over the Senate during the trial.

Two presidents have been impeached, Andrew Johnson in 1868, and William Jefferson Clinton in 1998. Neither was convicted. Richard Milhous Nixon faced almost certain impeachment in 1974, but resigned before articles of impeachment could be passed.

Section 4 Elections and Sessions

Clause 4.1 Elections

The Times, Places and Manner of holding Elections for Senators and Representatives, shall be prescribed in each State by the Legislature thereof; but the Congress may at any time by Law make or alter such Regulations, except as to the Places of chusing Senators.

State Versus Congressional Control Over Elections

This clause sets up a never-ending battle between state and federal power. The Supreme Court also weighed in on the question of fair election rules, especially under the 14th Amendment's guarantee of equal protection of the laws, and after the Voting Rights Act of 1965.

Clause 4.2 Sessions of Congress

The Congress shall assemble at least once in every Year, and such Meeting shall be on the first Monday in December unless they shall by Law appoint a different Day.

"on the first Monday in December"

The 20th Amendment, Section 2 changed this date to January 3 to better fit with the new swearing-in dates of President and Vice President (January 20).

18

Section 5 Internal Organization

Clause 5.1 Quorum, Attendance, Seating

Each House shall be the Judge of the Elections, Returns and Qualifications of its own Members, and a Majority of each shall constitute a Quorum to do Business; but a smaller Number may adjourn from day to day, and may be authorized to compel the Attendance of absent Members, in such Manner, and under such Penalties as each House may provide.

Clause 5.2 Rules, Punishment, Expulsion

Each House may determine the Rules of its Proceedings, punish its Members for disorderly Behaviour, and, with the Concurrence of two thirds, expel a Member.

Bylaws to Govern Congress

Congress is largely free to develop rules regarding member conduct.

Expulsion of a Member

Powell v. McCormack (1969) ruled that Congress could only expel a member by an explicit 2/3 vote. Congress could only expel members if they failed to meet citizenship, age, and residency requirements already listed. Until that point, Congress occasionally refused to seat members for a variety of reasons, including conviction for crimes.

Clause 5.3 Openness, Secrecy, Roll Call Votes

Each House shall keep a Journal of its Proceedings, and from time to time publish the same, excepting such Parts as may in their Judgment require Secrecy; and the Yeas and Nays of the Members of either House on any question shall, at the Desire of one fifth of those Present, be entered on the Journal.

Section 5 Internal Organization, Cont'd

"Journal of its Proceedings"

The Journals list votes held, and when a fifth of those present demand it, a roll call vote. The roll call vote puts each Senator or Representative on record and given the difficulty of the process, also serves to delay proceedings.

"Secrecy"

The Framers wished House and Senate to be able to debate freely, but they had no wish to create a ruling cabal The House made its sessions open, except for special purposes. The Senate has been more secretive, keeping its sessions closed until the 1790s, and keeping committee meetings closed until the rule reforms of the mid-1970s.

Congressional Record

The *Congressional Record* includes debates and statements entered into the record. Be forewarned, however that Representatives and Senators retain the right to edit their remarks before publication, so what you read may not be precisely what they said.

> **Clause 5.4 Adjournment and Place of Meeting**
> Neither House, during the Session of Congress, shall, without the Consent of the other, adjourn for more than three days, nor to any other Place than that in which the two Houses shall be sitting.

Adjournment

House and Senate must agree on a date of adjournment to end a given legislative session. Both have the independent power to end their sessions for the day or for up to three days. They are not permitted to independently move the seat of government. If they cannot agree to a time of adjournment, the President may adjourn them, though no President has ever done so. See 2.3.1a below.

Section 6 Compensation and Limits

Clause 6.1 Payment and Immunities

The Senators and Representatives shall receive a Compensation for their Services, to be ascertained by Law, and paid out of the Treasury of the United States. They shall in all Cases, except Treason, Felony and Breach of the Peace, be privileged from Arrest during their Attendance at the Session of their respective Houses, and in going to and returning from the same; and for any Speech or Debate in either House, they shall not be questioned in any other Place.

"Compensation. . . Treasury of the United States"

Pay for Congress is determined by law. The point here is that they are not paid by state treasuries, as they had been under the Articles. Congress not only represents the states, but the nation. The 27th Amendment prevents a Congress from raising its own pay, though it can raise the pay of the Congress that follows it.

"privileged from arrest during their Attendance"

There is little to this privilege. Members are still liable for any crime worth bragging about. They can be sued during a session.

"privileged from arrest. . . for any Speech or Debate"

Congressmen cannot be sued for libel for anything they say when doing the work of legislating. They can, however, be sued for statements made outside of that narrow function. Nor may any of their legislative functions be used as evidence against them in any court proceedings.

Section 6 Compensation and Limits, Cont'd

Clause 6.2 Incompatibility and Emoluments

No Senator or Representative shall, during the Time for which he was elected, be appointed to any civil Office under the Authority of the United States, which shall have been created, or the Emoluments whereof shall have been encreased during such time; and no Person holding any Office under the United States, shall be a Member of either House during his Continuance in Office.

Emoluments Clause

No Senator or Representative may be appointed to any office created while he or she was in office, or to any office that had increased its pay, pensions, or other "emoluments" during that period.

Incompatibility Clause

Legislators may not hold any other federal offices while in office. They cannot be military officers, for example, or serve in both houses, or serve as judges, federal bureaucrats, or as elected officials such as President. The point of this provision was to maintain the separation of powers between the branches of government, and to prevent favored lawmakers from receiving lucrative make-work jobs. Spouses and relatives of lawmakers may take jobs in the Executive branch, but scandals have arisen when such jobs have proved to be obviously fake.

Work-Arounds

There have been cases where lawmakers have been appointed to jobs for which the Congress had just raised the pay. In such cases, Presidents have requested that the pay be lowered for the new appointee to the old level in order to comply with this provision.

Section 7 Lawmaking Process

> **Clause 7.1 Tax Laws**
> All Bills for raising Revenue shall originate in the House of Representatives; but the Senate may propose or concur with Amendments as on other Bills.

All Tax Bills Must Begin in the House

This provision was originally conceived as part of the Great Compromise See 1.1.1. It was intended to be a sop to the larger-population states that (it was assumed) would dominate in the House. It might have had slightly more impact in its original form, when the Senate was also prohibited from adding amendments to revenue bills.

What Power Does the House Gain from This?

Little or none. There isn't much practical difference between originating a bill, after all, and adding an amendment. In practice, the House and Senate negotiate revenue-raising bills in largely the same manner as any other bill. It is more important as an artifact of how the Founding Fathers worked out the relative functions of House and Senate. (Elbridge Gerry referred to this issue in a letter, January 21, 1788, *Farrands*, III, 263)

Section 7 Lawmaking Process, Cont'd

Clause 7.2 Presentment Clause

Every Bill which shall have passed the House of Representatives and the Senate, shall, before it becomes a Law, be presented to the President of the United States; If he approve he shall sign it, but if not he shall return it, with his Objections to that House in which it shall have originated, who shall enter the Objections at large on their Journal, and proceed to reconsider it. If after such Reconsideration two thirds of that House shall agree to pass the Bill, it shall be sent, together with the Objections, to the other House, by which it shall likewise be reconsidered, and if approved by two thirds of that House, it shall become a Law. But in all such Cases the Votes of both Houses shall be determined by yeas and Nays, and the Names of the Persons voting for and against the Bill shall be entered on the Journal of each House respectively. If any Bill shall not be returned by the President within ten Days (Sundays excepted) after it shall have been presented to him, the Same shall be a Law, in like Manner as if he had signed it, unless the Congress by their Adjournment prevent its Return, in which Case it shall not be a Law.

Veto and Difficulty of Passing Bills

Keep in mind the difficulty of passing a bill through the procedures of both houses then reconciling the two versions. Because of this, the veto returns a bill to the final voting stage. It can be quickly passed by 2/3 vote overriding the veto. Or not.

Pocket Passage

If the president fails to sign a bill while Congress is in session it becomes a law after 10 days.

Section 7 Lawmaking Process, Cont'd

Pocket Veto

If a bill is passed so late that Congress adjourns before the 10 days is up, the President can ignore it. In such a case the bill does *not* become law, and Congress has to wait until its next session, and then be forced to start the entire lengthy process over again (unlike in a normal veto).

Pro Forma Sessions

To prevent pocket vetoes, (and to prevent the President from making "recess appointments" without the "Advice and Consent" of the Senate), Congress stayed in "pro forma" session starting during George W. Bush's presidency even when members were not actually doing work.

Line Item Veto

The Court ruled that the President may not decide to accept part of some laws and not others. Therefore, the so-called "line item veto" was ruled unconstitutional. See *Clinton v. City of New York* (1998)

Presidential Signing Statements

In these statements, Presidents can give their interpretation of a law, including whether or not they consider aspects to be unconstitutional, and the extent to which they intend to enforce the law. The Court has yet to rule definitively on the extent to which these statements conform to or violate the Presentment clause. Are they like a line item veto in that they approve part of a bill and not another? Are they examples of Presidential lawmaking? Or are they simply notice of Presidential intentions as regards how he or she will "faithfully execute" the laws? Prior to George W. Bush's Presidency, such statements mostly served as a sort of flourish. They were exceeding rare until Ronald Reagan's presidency.

Section 7 Lawmaking Process, Cont'd

Clause 7.3 All Bills, Full Legislative Process

Every Order, Resolution, or Vote to which the Concurrence of the Senate and House of Representatives may be necessary (except on a question of Adjournment) shall be presented to the President of the United States; and before the Same shall take Effect, shall be approved by him, or being disapproved by him, shall be repassed by two thirds of the Senate and House of Representatives, according to the Rules and Limitations prescribed in the Case of a Bill.

"Every Order..."
(Primacy of Legislative Process)

In this complex section the Framers attempted to ensure that all federal authority would be exercised *only* by going through the entire legislative process. They wished to prevent both Congress and the President from bypassing checks and balances. The vast expansion of government institutional power in the Congressional and Presidentially-controlled bureaucracy has tested this clause to the limit.

Section 8 Enumerated Powers

Clause 8.1 Taxes, Debt, Welfare, Uniformity

The Congress shall have Power To lay and collect Taxes, Duties, Imposts and Excises, to pay the Debts and provide for the common Defence and general Welfare of the United States; but all Duties, Imposts and Excises shall be uniform throughout the United States;

Enumerated Powers

This is the name given to the 18 powers "enumerated" (listed) in Section 1.8. "Strict Construction" thinkers such as Thomas Jefferson insisted that these were properly the *only* powers ceded to Congress. All others should be reserved to the states (see 10th Amendment). "Loose Construction" thinkers such as Alexander Hamilton disagreed.

Section 8 Enumerated Powers, Cont'd

Loose Construction

See "Elastic Clause" (1.8.18). In practice, in order for Congress to accomplish the goals of the first 17 powers listed, it claimed the right to do whatever was "necessary and proper" to accomplish them.

"lay and collect Taxes"

This addressed a major limit on the power of the national government under the Articles. Under the Articles, the national government depended on the state governments to pay their portion of taxes, but with no mechanism to force them to do so. Under the Constitution, the national government could enact taxes on individuals of the states.

"shall be uniform"

Clause 1.2.3 required taxes to be apportioned evenly according to population among the states. See also 16th Amendment legalizing federal income taxes that overturned this clause. This clause should underline the more state-oriented nature of the Constitution when passed. See Capitation Tax and Direct Tax, 1.9.4.

> **Clause 8.2 Congress and Credit**
> To borrow Money on the credit of the United States;

Congress's Power to Borrow

The new nation needed the kind of credit that it had never established under the Articles. Alexander Hamilton hoped to use payment of the Revolutionary War debt to help concentrate the nation's sparse wealth in order to create investment capital. This policy recreated the situation that had motivated rural Pennsylvania to join the Revolution and helped to create the Whiskey Rebellion in the 1790s.

Section 8 Enumerated Powers, Cont'd

Clause 8.3 Commerce Clause

To regulate Commerce with foreign Nations, and among the several States, and with the Indian Tribes;

Commerce Clause

Congress has the right to regulate commerce. What kinds? To what extent? What, for example, is the difference between Congress taking property (forbidden under 5th Amendment) and regulating commerce? It's complicated.

Outline of Commerce Clause

1. With Foreign Nations
2. Among the States
   a) Broad Authority to Congress (Early National)
   b) Contradictory Precedents (Gilded/Progressive Era)
      i)   Indirect Commerce (Manufacturing, Mining)
      ii) Stream of Commerce (Stockyards, Railroads)
      iii) No Social Legislation (Wages and Hours)
   c) Almost Unlimited Power Over Commerce (New Deal)
      i) Labor Unions
      ii) As Authority for Civil Rights Laws
   d) Re-limited (Post-1995)
3. With Indian Tribes

1. With Foreign Nations

See 2.2.2 for the President's power to make treaties with the advice and consent of the Senate. The key here is that commerce with foreign nations was a matter for the national government, not the states.

Section 8 Enumerated Powers, Cont'd

2. Among the States

When does commerce in one state touch on the commerce of another state *enough* to qualify as "among the several States"? At the least, the answer has changed with technology: Horses, canal boats, steamboats, railroads, telegraphs, trucks, and Internet connected the commerce of the several states in fundamentally different ways.

The answer changed with the nature of the economy and the balance of federalism. In the Early National period, the Marshall Court sought to expand federal authority into the prerogatives of the states. During the Gilded Age (roughly 1870-1900), judges sought to block most Congressional economic regulations. In the New Deal era (1937-1941), the Court gave Congress almost unlimited economic power.

a) Broad Authority to Congress (Early National)

The Court defined commerce relatively broadly in early cases. In *Gibbons v. Ogden* (1824), it ruled that New York could not grant a monopoly to a steamboat company. It focused on preventing states from interfering in commercial activity, especially (as in *Gibbons*) commercial activity that Congress had authorized, and that crossed state lines. The Federalist Marshall Court wished to expand national power.

b) Contradictory Precedents (Gilded/Progressive Era)

Commerce at the dawn of the 1900s connected states and nation in ways that the Framers in 1787 never expected. In response, the Court developed three contradictory sets of precedents. In the New Deal era, it would expand the second of these, allowing most economic regulations.

i) *Indirect Commerce (Manufacturing, Mining)* It prohibited regulation of business "indirectly" related to interstate commerce. *US v. EC Knight* (1895). Congress could not regulate sugar refining (nor mines or factories). See also *Carter v. Carter Coal Co.* (1936)

29

Section 8 Enumerated Powers, Cont'd

ii) *Stream of Commerce (Stockyards, Railroads)* It let Congress regulate some forms of commercial activity, even within a state (Chicago stockyards, *Swift v. US* (1905)) and railroads, *Shreveport Rate Case* (1914)) that it saw as part of the "stream of commerce." *Interstate Commerce Commission v. Atchison T & SF R. Co.* (1893)

iii) *No Social Legislation (Wages and Hours)* The Court continued to be suspicious of regulations that seemed to go outside the narrow economic purposes, invalidating a ban on child labor. *Hammer v. Dagenhart* (1918). (See also 14th Amendment, Substantive Due Process, and *Lochner v. New York* (1905)).

c) Almost Unlimited Authority to Congress: New Deal

In 1937, the Court deferred more to Congress's judgment in making economic regulations with its decision in *National Labor Relations Board v. Jones & McLaughlin Steel* (1937). Between 1937-1995, the Court allowed Congress to regulate business under the Commerce Clause.

i) *Labor Unions: Collective Worker Rights and Collective Property Rights* The National Labor Relations Act, or "Wagner Act" passed in 1935 legalized union activism—narrowly—for the first time. Unions had long existed, but Common Law limited what they could do. The Court's narrow interpretation of the Commerce Clause prohibited federal laws regulating labor in the "laissez faire" era prior to 1937. The Court's "Liberty of Contract" also prohibited state laws regulating labor in this era. Employers could evade state laws limiting hours, conditions of work, or safety regulations by having workers sign a contract waiving such protections. Employment contracts could include clauses prohibiting union membership or requiring workers to join company unions. The Wagner Act regulated labor unions and required companies to negotiate with them in good faith.

Section 8 Enumerated Powers, Cont'd

Prior to the Wagner Act almost all labor union activism was prohibited as illegal conspiracy to intimidate under Common Law. The first effective precedent was *Commonwealth v. Pullis* (1806) (The "Cordwainers Case"). The second major precedent was *Commonwealth v. Hunt* (1842), an influential Massachusetts opinion written by leading justice Lemuel Shaw. Gilded Age judges routinely issued injunctions prohibiting picketing, strikes, and nearly all strike-related union activities. Such injunctions were prohibited by the Norris-LaGuardia Act (1932).

ii) *As Authority for Civil Rights laws* Congress used the Commerce Clause to justify its power to pass the Civil Rights Act of 1964 that prohibited racial discrimination in private enterprises. (See 14th Amendment narrowing of privileges & immunities for why Congress couldn't directly claim the power to outlaw racial discrimination.) See *Hearts of Atlanta Motel v. US* (1964).

3. With Indian Tribes

This clause sees the Indian Tribes as political entities with semi-sovereign rights—as "domestic dependent nations." See *Cherokee Nation v. Georgia* (1831) that gave Indians few rights that Georgia had to respect, and *Worcester v. Georgia* (1832) that voided Georgian laws on Cherokee land (Georgia and President Andrew Jackson ignored the Court. For impact, see "Trail of Tears.")

Section 8 Enumerated Powers, Cont'd

Clause 8.4 Naturalization, Bankruptcy
To establish an uniform Rule of Naturalization, and uniform Laws on the subject of Bankruptcies throughout the United States;

Uniform Rules for Naturalization and Bankruptcies

The emphasis is on national standards for citizenship and treatment of debtors across all states. Congress first created a bankruptcy act in 1898, with major amendments in 1938 and 1978. It passed a naturalization act in 1790 that allowed only free whites to be naturalized. The 14th Amendment established citizenship for "all persons" born in America.

Clause 8.5 Money, Standard Weights and Measures
To coin Money, regulate the Value thereof, and of foreign Coin, and fix the Standard of Weights and Measures;

"To coin Money"

The Constitution includes a more sophisticated set of federal monetary powers than implied by this clause alone. It appeared to straightforwardly limit Congress to regulating the quantity and quality of precious metal in silver and gold coin. But in combination with the Commerce Clause (1.8.3), and the power to borrow money (1.8.2) it also gave Congress the power to issue paper money, and to require its acceptance as legal tender.

Clause 8.6 Counterfeiting
To provide for the Punishment of counterfeiting the Securities and current Coin of the United States;

Section 8 Enumerated Powers, Cont'd

Counterfeiting

The power to regulate commerce and money makes necessary the power to prevent counterfeiting.

Clause 8.7 Post Offices and Post Roads

To establish Post Offices and post Roads;

1st Amendment Versus Congressional Power

Congress argued that the power to establish Post Offices gave it the right to forbid mailing subversive or salacious materials. It applied this power freely, especially during and after World War I. See *US ex rel Milwaukee Social Democratic Publishing Co. v. Burleson* (1921). In *Hannegan v. Esquire* (1946) the Court ruled that 1st Amendment freedom of speech forbids Congress from using this power to impose its taste.

Mail Fraud

Congress may prohibit use of the mail for fraud. *Public Clearing House v. Coyne* (1904).

Pullman Strike

When a railroad strike happened to stop the US mail, the Court allowed a federal injunction under this power against the entire strike effort. *In re Debs* (1895).

Clause 8.8 Copyright

To promote the Progress of Science and useful Arts, by securing for limited Times to Authors and Inventors the exclusive Right to their respective Writings and Discoveries;

Section 8 Enumerated Powers, Cont'd

Copyright, Patent, Trademark

The point of this clause is named in the first few words: "To promote the Progress. . ." Congress has broad power to promote creative efforts by giving creators a set of exclusive rights. The Court's involvement has largely been limited to defining what is meant by the key terms: Promotion, progress, invention, and discovery.

Clause 8.9 Inferior Courts
To constitute Tribunals inferior to the supreme Court;

Article 1 Courts

This clause gives Congress the power to set up temporary and/or specialized courts. These "Article 1 Courts" have judges who serve for specific terms rather than for life.

Clause 8.10 High Seas and Laws of Nations
To define and punish Piracies and Felonies committed on the high Seas, and Offenses against the Law of Nations;

Plenary Power

Congress has been granted this power exclusively in part so that individual states will not take it upon themselves to set up separate rules.

International Law

This clause gives Congress the power to set up courts to try violations of international law such as the laws of war.

Clause 8.11 To Declare War
To declare War, grant Letters of Marque and Reprisal, and make Rules concerning Captures on Land and Water;

Section 8 Enumerated Powers, Cont'd

"To declare War"

The Court has refused to referee in the battle between the President's executive function as Commander in Chief of the armed forces, and Congress's power to formally declare war. In practice, Presidents generally make war as an extension of their power over foreign affairs, and dare Congress to stop them, mostly through its control over revenues necessary to deploy the armed forces.

"grant Letters of Marque and Reprisal"

This clause grants Congress the sole right to issue what were essentially licenses for piracy or "privateers" beyond the "Marque" or border of the nation. A common practice in the 18th century, this is no longer a legal practice under international law. (Congress issued such a letter during World War II to allow blimps to patrol for submarines.)

"To. . . make Rules concerning Captures

This clause allows Congress sole right to make rules for seizing enemy property.

Clause 8.12 Army

To raise and support Armies, but no Appropriation of Money to that Use shall be for a longer Term than two Years;

Clause 8.13 Navy

To provide and maintain a Navy;

Clause 8.14 Military Code

To make Rules for the Government and Regulation of the land and naval Forces;

Section 8 Enumerated Powers, Cont'd

"To raise and support Armies"

This clause gives Congress the right to impose a draft (as the states did under the Articles). The limit of two years on appropriations addresses the fear of standing armies.

"To make Rules. . . for the land and naval Forces"

The military has separate judicial processes.

Navy

The Navy was seen as less dangerous to liberties than a standing army, and more in need of long-term investment.

Clause 8.15 Control of Militia

To provide for calling forth the Militia to execute the Laws of the Union, suppress Insurrections and repel Invasions;

Clause 8.16 Division of Militia with States

To provide for organizing, arming, and disciplining, the Militia, and for governing such Part of them as may be employed in the Service of the United States, reserving to the States respectively, the Appointment of the Officers, and the Authority of training the Militia according to the discipline prescribed by Congress;

Control of Militia

These two clauses give Congress some power over the individual state militias. The 2nd Amendment reassured the states that this clause was not a sneaky means of consolidating armed power in national hands.

Section 8 Enumerated Powers, Cont'd

> **Clause 8.17 District of Columbia**
>
> To exercise exclusive Legislation in all Cases whatsoever, over such District (not exceeding ten Miles square) as may, by Cession of particular States, and the Acceptance of Congress, become the Seat of the Government of the United States, and to exercise like Authority over an Places purchased by the Consent of the Legislature of the State in which the Same shall be, for the Erection of Forts, Magazines, Arsenals, dockyards and other needful Buildings;

Washington, District of Columbia

The District of Columbia was first established by Congress in 1790. The decision to create a separate District gave the new Federal Government independence from the states. It was located in Virginia as part of the compromise that nationalized state Revolutionary War debts.

Self-Government in Washington, DC

This increasingly large city slowly gained powers of self-government since 1967. It has one Delegate, but no *voting* representation in Congress. Its residents were first able to vote for President through the 23rd Amendment (1961).

> **Clause 8.18 Necessary and Proper**
>
> And To make all Laws which shall be necessary and proper for carrying into Execution the foregoing Powers, and all other Powers vested by this Constitution in the Government of the United States or in any Department or Officer thereof.

Section 8 Enumerated Powers, Cont'd

Necessary and Proper, Elastic, Coefficient Clause

This clause expands federal power by allowing Congress to pass any laws that it deems necessary to enact the preceding list of Enumerated Powers.

Strict Construction: Necessary and Proper

One view of this clause sees it as strictly limiting federal power. Thomas Jefferson, a proponent of limited national power insisted to George Washington that this clause allowed Congress to make *only* those laws that were both necessary *and* proper. That is, he saw "absolutely" implied before the word "necessary," and the words "for survival" after it. This view would have limited Congress's powers to those "expressly" enumerated, as in the Articles.

Loose Construction

Alexander Hamilton's interpretation came to rule, mostly. He insisted to George Washington that the term "necessary and proper" did not limit the power of Congress, but rather expanded it to any laws implied by the foregoing Enumerated Powers. Thus, this clause came to be called "elastic" because it could be broadly interpreted by Congress to include powers not specifically mentioned, but important to carrying out enumerated powers. "Necessary" here means whatever powers were needed in order to accomplish the functions of government authorized by the Constitution. As with so much in the Constitution, the clause's elasticity depends on the political power and restraint of those doing the stretching.

Section 8 Enumerated Powers, Cont'd

Court's Ruling on Necessary and Proper

In *McCulloch v. Maryland* (1819), the Court agreed with
Hamilton. It ruled that the term "necessary and proper" gave
Congress the power to make laws implied by the foregoing powers.
It ruled that the enumerated powers allowing Congress to regulate
Interstate Commerce, raise taxes and borrow implied the power to
create a national bank. Moreover, combined with the Supremacy
Clause, such a power made Maryland's law taxing the National
Bank Branch in Baltimore unconstitutional.

Section 9 Limits on Congress

Clause 9.1 Right to Slave Trade

The Migration or Importation of such Persons as any of the
States now existing shall think proper to admit, shall not be
prohibited by the Congress prior to the Year one thousand
eight hundred and eight, but a Tax or duty may be imposed on
such Importation, not exceeding ten dollars for each Person.

State Power to Continue Importing Slaves

In this clause, "such Persons" refers to slaves. As soon as permitted
by the Constitution, in 1808, Congress prohibited importation of
slaves (though enforcement was spotty at best, impeded as it was by
state officials sympathetic to the slave trade, and an executive little
interested in stopping it.)

Section 9 Limits on Congress, Cont'd

> **Clause 9.2 Habeas Corpus**
> The Privilege of the Writ of Habeas Corpus shall not be sus-
> pended, unless when in Cases of Rebellion or Invasion the
> public Safety may require it.

Habeas Corpus

Latin for "have the body." Despite being written during a time
when all lawyers were expected to have a working knowledge
of Latin (and Greek), the Constitution is notable for its lack of
obscure Latin legalisms. The use of Habeas Corpus should be a clue
to the term's familiarity. It named a basic right ("The Great Writ")
hallowed by its antiquity in English law. It was the right to freedom
from arbitrary seizure, or jailing without due process. It gives prisoners the right to have their imprisonment justified before a judge.

"Cases of Rebellion or Invasion"

Early in the Civil War Abraham Lincoln suspended the right of
Habeas Corpus, as did Ulysses S. Grant in battling the Ku Klux Klan.

Habeas Corpus Today

Recently, the Court has reasserted its right to review the US government's reasons for holding any and all prisoners. The problem
has been raised in the context of people imprisoned for terrorist
acts, sometimes overseas, and sometimes without trial. See *Hamdi
v. Rumsfeld* (2004), *Hamdan v. Rumsfeld* (2006), and *Boumediene v.
Bush* (2008).

Suspension of Habeas Corpus

The location of this clause suggests that this power belongs to
Congress. But in practice, crises that may require suspension sel-
dom lend themselves to Congress's pace. Who gets to decide when
it's OK for the government to snatch whomever it wishes and put
that person in jail without trial? Who decides when that period is

Section 9 Limits on Congress, Cont'd

over? In practice this is a question to be battled out between the three branches. Congress's role has typically been to either endorse Presidential action, to limit it, or to bring the period of suspension to an end.

> **Clause 9.3 Bill of Attainder, Ex Post Facto**
> No Bill of Attainder or ex post facto Law shall be passed.

"Bill of Attainder"

This refers to laws that single out individuals or easily-identified groups for punishment without trial. Think of the root word "taint." Often used to condemn entire family line—see "corruption of blood" under limits on Congress, 3.3.2

"ex post facto Law"

Again, the Latin here "after the fact" referred to a familiar legal concept. People cannot be punished under criminal law for acts that were legal when they did them.

> **Clause 9.4 Capitation Tax**
> No Capitation, or other direct, Tax shall be laid, unless in Proportion to the Census or Enumeration herein before directed to be taken.

"No Capitation, or other direct, Tax unless in Proportion"

A capitation tax is a uniform tax on each person, or person within a category (Adult men, slaves, left-handed history professors, etc.). This clause prevented Congress from levying a capitation tax on a type of person concentrated in a single section of the country (southern slaves), and incidentally, land. It was made obsolete by the 16th Amendment.

41

Section 9 Limits on Congress, Cont'd

"or other direct, Tax"

From debates at the Convention, it seems to refer to taxing the
states "directly" in a way that might burden one or more out of proportion with their level of political representation. (For example,
a tax of $1.00 per acre of land would have vastly more impact in
North Carolina than in Connecticut.) They were not trying to
protect individuals but states. The Court defined "direct" taxes
to be only capitation/head taxes (say, on slaves) or taxes on land.
(When Rufus King, Constitutional Convention delegate from
Massachusetts demanded its precise meaning: "No one answd."
(August 20, 1787. Farrand II, 350.))

> **Clause 9.5 Export Taxes on a State**
> No Tax or Duty shall be laid on Articles exported from any
> State.

This is the 2nd of 3 clauses, as with 1.9.4, and 1.9.6 that prevent
Congress from unfairly burdening one state or section to benefit
the others. At the time of passage, some states exported far more
than others. The Southern slave states in particular depended more
on exports than on internal trade for their prosperity.

> **Clause 9.6 State Ports**
> No Preference shall be given by any Regulation of
> Commerce or Revenue to the Ports of one State over those
> of another: nor shall Vessels bound to, or from, one State,
> be obliged to enter, clear, or pay Duties in another.

This clause prevents individual states from receiving preferential
treatment from Congress. It also prevents states from taxing interstate commerce. See also Commerce Clause 1.8.3 above.

Section 9 Limits on Congress, Cont'd

> **Clause 9.7 Appropriations by Law Only**
> No Money shall be drawn from the Treasury, but in Consequence of Appropriations made by Law, and a regular Statement and Account of the Receipts and Expenditures of all public Money shall be published from time to time.

"No Money shall be drawn from the Treasury"

This is a somewhat oddly placed clause since it is most often seen as a limitation on the Executive. The President cannot spend any money without authorization by a law. But it is also a limitation on Congress given that it requires that expenditures go through the entire legislative process in both houses, and that accounts be published.

"shall be published from time to time"

Originally, the Framers had required that such accounts be published annually, but they were concerned that Congress might ignore such a specific requirement if it were inconvenient in any given year.

> **Clause 9.8 Titles and Emoluments**
> No Title of Nobility shall be granted by the United States: And no Person holding any Office of Profit or Trust under them, shall, without the Consent of the Congress, accept of any present, Emolument, Office, or Title, of any kind what-ever, from any King, Prince, or foreign State.

To modern ears, this clause may seem unnecessary. Why not allow Congress to bestow an honorific title on a citizen? Why not allow a US government official to accept title from a foreign government? But such titles at this time were not simple honorifics, but implied creation of a special class, with inherited status.

Section 10 Limits on States

> **Clause 10.1 No state shall...**
>
> No State shall enter into any Treaty, Alliance, or Confederation; grant Letters of Marque and Reprisal; coin Money; emit Bills of Credit; make any Thing but gold and silver Coin a Tender in Payment of Debts; pass any Bill of Attainder, ex post facto Law, or Law impairing the Obligation of Contracts, or grant any Title of Nobility.

Limits on State Sovereignty

The limits on state power often overlap with the limits on Congress. The point of these clauses was to give substance to the Supremacy Clause that made the Constitution the supreme law of the land.

Until the Court began to rule that the 14th Amendment "incorporated" some of the Bill of Rights such as Freedom of Speech, this was the main section of the Constitution that limited state actions. Nor, at the time that the Framers wrote this, did they plan on adding the Bill of Rights. They assumed most personal rights would be ensured by state governments. This section therefore listed the limits to state sovereignty that the Framers thought most important to creating a true national government. It also listed a few of the limits they thought most important to ensure democratic national government—such as limits on Bills of Attainder, Ex Post Facto laws, breaking contracts, and Noble titles.

"No State shall enter into any Treaty"

Only Congress can make laws regarding relations with other countries.

"No State shall coin Money"

Only Congress may manage the money supply. This is a major difference from the Articles.

Section 10 Limits on States, Cont'd

"No State shall...pass any Bill of Attainder, [or] ex post facto Law"

States may pass no laws aimed at specific individuals or groups. Nor may the states punish acts that were legal when done. (Congress is also prohibited from passing such laws. See clause 1.9.3 above.)

"No State shall...pass any... law impairing...Contracts"

Early on, the Court used this clause to protect contracts from states. See *Fletcher v. Peck* (1810) and *Dartmouth College v. Woodward* (1819). Later, the Court allowed states to balance this guarantee against the public good ("police power"). For example, even if the state granted a corporate charter for selling alcohol, it could outlaw alcohol sales if it believed that doing so was good for the state. See *Boston Beer Co. v. Massachusetts* (1878). In the 1930s, the Court allowed states to relieve mortgage obligations. Much later, it created a set of rules for applying this clause. See *Home Building & Loan Association v. Blaisdell* (1934) and *Energy Reserves Group v. Kansas Power & Light* (1983).

"No State shall...grant any Title of Nobility"

Such laws granting special legal status to individuals were forbidden to both Congress and the States. See the "Emoluments Clause" 1.6.2.

Clause 10.2 No State Taxes on Interstate Commerce

No State shall, without the Consent of the Congress, lay any Imposts or Duties on Imports or Exports, except what may be absolutely necessary for executing it's inspection Laws: and the net Produce of all Duties and Imposts, laid by any State on Imports or Exports, shall be for the Use of the Treasury of the United States; and all such Laws shall be subject to the Revision and Controul of the Congress.

Section 10 Limits on States, Cont'd

"No State shall....lay any...Duties on Imports or Exports

The "import-export" clause eliminated barriers to interstate trade, and reinforced Congress's role as the sole source of interstate regulations. It does not exempt imported goods from state sales taxes after they have been imported and made available for sale. See 21st Amendment, Section 2.

> **Clause 10.3 No Port Taxes and Standing Armies**
>
> No State shall, without the Consent of Congress, lay any Duty of Tonnage, keep Troops, or Ships of War in time of Peace, enter into any Agreement or Compact with another State, or with a foreign Power, or engage in War, unless actually invaded, or in such imminent Danger as will not admit of delay.

"No State shall...lay any Duty of Tonnage"

Ensures that the federal government had sole control over management of imports and foreign policy.

"No State shall...enter into any...Compact"

Prevents states from conspiring to undermine the national government. They may make "Interstate Compacts" regarding basic issues such as borders, transportation, etc.

"...with a foreign power]"

Control over foreign policy and warfare is reserved for the federal government unless the state is invaded.

Article 2 Executive (President)

A strain of Revolutionary thought insisted that Americans needed no single executive. The Articles had had none. The Framers' main model for such an executive position was that of the Constitutional monarch of Great Britain, and they had no wish to create a new sort of King.

The Framers had long experience with the theory and practice of legislatures. Not so with the Executive.

One important constraint on the President that appears nowhere in the text has been self-restraint and respect for tradition. Presidents have tended to consult Congress and obey the Supreme Court's edicts.

Except when they don't. In times of crisis, Presidents have focused on action over deliberation. Executive crises since Theodore Roosevelt's time have come thicker and faster. Since World War II they seem nearly constant.

It has been an ongoing struggle: Presidents have sought to expand Executive capacity to preside over a world of complexity and speed never envisioned by the Framers—while Congress and the Court have sought to keep it safely bound down by checks and balances. (Congress has also increased its staffing to keep up with the complexity and capacity of the executive branch.)

The President has only a few Enumerated Powers:

1. Appoint judges, ambassadors, other officials.
2. Commander in Chief of the Military.
3. Make treaties.
4. Grant pardons.

All the rest are implied Executive Powers, and powers Presidents have taken because they could.

Section 1 Terms and Electors

> **Clause 1.1 Executive Power and President**
> The executive Power shall be vested in a President of the United States of America. He shall hold his Office during the Term of four Years, and, together with the Vice President, chosen for the same Term, be elected, as follows

"The executive Power shall be vested in a President"

Given the lack of enumerated restrictions below some "Unitary Executive" theorists argue that presidents may exercise all powers that may be defined as "executive" without limit. In practice, the President's powers, as with those of Congress and the Courts, have been limited by tradition, self-restraint, and the power of the other branches.

Congressional Acquiescence

This legal doctrine explains the limits to Presidential power by the limits to what Congress can legislate and investigate. The Court has largely refused to referee between Executive and Congress unless Congress has taken clear action. See *Youngstown Sheet & Tube v. Sawyer* (1952) for an example of the Court siding with Congress against President Harry Truman.

Congressional Limits on Executive Power

The limit is largely practical. Congress struggles to deliberate in a manner sufficient to challenge modern Presidents on quickly-unfolding issues. Add to this the modern-day problem of almost constant fund-raising and staff limitations (Members of Congress typically schedule meetings on Tuesdays, Wednesdays, and Thursdays since members must travel to their districts so much of the time.) Congress has become increasingly like a Board of Directors facing off against a wily Chief Executive Officer and his or her vast staff.

Section 1 Terms and Electors, Cont'd

> **Clause 1.2 Selecting Electors**
> Each State shall appoint, in such Manner as the Legislature thereof may direct, a Number of Electors, equal to the whole Number of Senators and Representatives to which the State may be entitled in the Congress: but no Senator or Representative, or Person holding an Office of Trust or Profit under the United States, shall be appointed an Elector.

"Each State shall appoint"

State legislatures are responsible for controlling the selection of electors. While electors in some states retain the theoretical authority to change their votes, in practice they have very rarely done so.

Number of Electors

This number reflects the "Great Compromise" in which the people were represented both state-by-state and by population. Because of this, small-population states gained power over election of the President they otherwise would not have had. Prior to the end of slavery, this rule gave voters in slave-holding states 3/5 more power per slave. Ironically, emancipation gave the former slave states 1 full vote per non-white person rather than 3/5, even though prior to the Voting Rights Act of 1965, few of those non-white people could vote. See 14th Amendment, Section 2.

Section 1 Terms and Electors, Cont'd

Clause 1.3 Electoral College

The Electors shall meet in their respective States, and vote by Ballot for two Persons, of whom one at least shall not be an Inhabitant of the same State with themselves. And they shall make a List of all the Persons voted for, and of the Number of Votes for each; which List they shall sign and certify, and transmit sealed to the Seat of the Government of the United States, directed to the President of the Senate. The President of the Senate shall, in the Presence of the Senate and House of Representatives, open all the Certificates, and the Votes shall then be counted. The Person having the greatest Number of Votes shall be the President, if such Number be a Majority of the whole Number of Electors appointed; and if there be more than one who have such Majority, and have an equal Number of Votes, then the House of Representatives shall immediately chuse by Ballot one of them for President; and if no Person have a Majority, then from the five highest on the List the said House shall in like Manner chuse the President. But in chusing the President, the Votes shall be taken by States, the Representation from each State having one Vote; A quorum for this Purpose shall consist of a Member or Members from two thirds of the States, and a Majority of all the States shall be necessary to a Choice. In every Case, after the Choice of the President, the Person having the greatest Number of Votes of the Electors shall be the Vice President. But if there should remain two or more who have equal Votes, the Senate shall chuse from them by Ballot the Vice President.

Electoral College

This section has been replaced by the 12th Amendment. The explanation on the next page is therefore largely historical in nature. Go to the 12th Amendment to understand how the Electoral system works now.

Section 1 Terms and Electors, Cont'd

"one at least shall not be an Inhabitant of the same State with themselves"

The Framers were concerned that electors might only vote for residents of their own states.

Vice President

Originally the Vice President was to be the person with the second-highest number of electoral votes. This system became out-dated with the rise of Political Parties, and with the election of John Adams as President and his bitter political rival Thomas Jefferson as Vice President in 1796.

Clause 1.4 Election Day

The Congress may determine the Time of chusing the Electors, and the Day on which they shall give their Votes; which Day shall be the same throughout the United States.

"Time...of chusing the Electors"

The current law requires electors to be selected on the Tuesday after the first Monday in November.

"Day on which they shall give their votes"

The current law requires each state's electors to meet, to tabulate their votes, and send them to Washington on the first Monday after the second Wednesday in December.

Section 1 Terms and Electors, Cont'd

Clause 1.5 Eligibility to be President

No Person except a natural born Citizen, or a Citizen of the United States, at the time of the Adoption of this Constitution, shall be eligible to the Office of President; neither shall any person be eligible to that Office who shall not have attained to the Age of thirty five Years, and been fourteen Years a Resident within the United States.

"Natural born"

Legal technicalities aside, "Natural born" simply means "born an American citizen." The Court has never defined the precise meaning of this term for presidential candidates. (Had the Framers aimed to trip us up on technicalities, they had available Shakespeare's "of woman born.") The first presidents, of course, were citizens "at the time of the Adoption of this Constitution."

Faithless Electors

What if an elector insisted on voting against his or her instructions? While this has occurred on occasion, and there is no effective law forcing electors to vote as instructed, this has never been a significant problem in an election. Tradition and self-restraint have been sufficient up to this point.

"Shall be eligible"

The 20th Amendment, Section 1 provides that in case the President elect shall not be qualified, the Vice President elect shall take office until the President elect has qualified. This might suggest, though it has never been put to the test, that a president-elect who was under 35 could still be elected, but not take office until his or her birthday. I offer this to any presidential hopefuls who are sufficiently impatient and will be at least, say 33 years old by the time of the next Presidential Election.

Section 1 Terms and Electors, Cont'd

> **Clause 1.6 Line of Succession**
>
> In Case of the Removal of the President from Office, or of his Death, Resignation, or Inability to discharge the Powers and Duties of the said Office, the Same shall devolve on the Vice President, and the Congress may by Law provide for the Case of Removal, Death, Resignation or Inability, both of the President and Vice President, declaring what Officer shall then act as President, and such Officer shall act accordingly, until the Disability be removed, or a President shall be elected.

See 25th Amendment for new version of this clause.

"In Case of the Removal of the President…"

This rule of succession was not tested until 1841 when nominal Whig Party member John Tyler took over from deceased President William Henry Harrison and proceeded to upend the entire Whig platform.

"In Case of…Inability to discharge the Powers and Duties"

See 25th Amendment, passed in 1967. There is no better illustration of the changing nature of the world than the increasing urgency of making sure that there are no gaps in executive authority.

Line of Succession

Congress has created a definite line of succession in case of the death of President and Vice President at the same time. Indeed, the legal line of succession envisions the possibility of losing President, Vice President, Speaker of the House, President Pro Tempore of the Senate, Secretary of State, and successive Cabinet officers.

Section 1 Terms and Electors, Cont'd

> **Clause 1.7 Presidential Compensation**
> The President shall, at stated Times, receive for his Services, a Compensation, which shall neither be increased nor diminished during the Period for which he shall have been elected, and he shall not receive within that Period any other Emolument from the United States, or any of them.

"which shall neither be increased nor diminished"

Congress cannot raise or lower the President's pay during his time in office. This prevents Congress from bribing or penalizing the President. The last four words, "or any of them" prevents individual states from bribing the President.

> **Clause 1.8 Presidential Oath of Office**
> Before he enter on the Execution of his Office, he shall take the following Oath or Affirmation: "I do solemnly swear (or affirm) that I will faithfully execute the Office of President of the United States, and will to the best of my Ability, preserve, protect and defend the Constitution of the United States.

Who Administers the Oath?

By tradition, the Chief Justice of the Supreme Court administers the oath of office. Calvin Coolidge was sworn in by his father, a Notary Public in 1923. Lyndon Johnson was sworn in by Federal Judge Sarah T. Hughes after the assassination of John F. Kennedy in 1963.

"or Affirm"

Starting in the late 1600s, Quakers began to see oaths to tell the truth or to fulfill a promise as a suggestion that they might be untruthful in other contexts. Instead, such believers "affirmed" their truthfulness in this venue as in all others. This clause respects the distinction.

Section 2 Powers of the Executive

> ### Clause 2.1 Commander in Chief
>
> The President shall be Commander in Chief of the Army and Navy of the United States, and of the Militia of the several States, when called into the actual Service of the United States; he may require the Opinion, in writing, of the principal Officer in each of the executive Departments, upon any Subject relating to the Duties of their respective Offices,

Commander in Chief

National emergencies and the President's status as Commander in Chief of the military could put almost limitless power in the hands of the Executive who desired it. Nevertheless, the US has a strong tradition of restrained executives and resurgent Congresses when crises ebb. In this, George Washington remains the exemplar.

Unitary Executive

Starting in Ronald Reagan's terms of office (1980-1988), legal thinkers have argued that the President's power as Commander in Chief is plenary. That is, it is absolute and subject to few if any legal limitations from Congress. The Court has yet to rule definitively on this interpretation. It ultimately is a question of power among the branches of government as much as law. See "Executive Power and President" 2.1.1 above.

Executive Departments

The Constitution envisions advisors in a "cabinet." The term "cabinet" comes from the sense of a small room where advisors might meet (Compare to the "bureaucrats" who work for cabinet officers, the term originating in the French term for a desk.). Department heads must be approved with the "advice and consent" of the Senate, and their departments created and funded by laws.

Section 2 Powers of the Executive, Cont'd

> **Clause 2.1a, Cont'd Pardons**
> and he shall have Power to grant Reprieves and Pardons for Offenses against the United States, except in Cases of Impeachment.

"shall have Power"

The power to issue pardons implies the *lesser* power to issue partial pardons or reductions in punishment, the *greater* power to do so with conditions, and the *broader* power to issue amnesty to a class. For example, in 1974 President Gerald Ford offered a conditional pardon to men who had avoided the draft during the Vietnam War, and in 1977 President James Earl Carter granted a full pardon to all such men.

"Reprieves and Pardons for Offenses against the US"

A reprieve postpones punishment. A pardon ends or prevents punishment. As regards human citizens the president's pardon power is plenary—that is, complete. The tradition by which the President pardons a single turkey at Thanksgiving does not mean he can pardon all turkeys; they are privately owned and neither persons nor citizens.

"against the United States"

Such powers apply only to federal crimes, not crimes against states or in civil lawsuits. So the President can't get you out of a speeding ticket (state or municipal law), resolve your divorce (civil), or change your grade in class.

"except in Cases of Impeachment"

The President cannot use a pardon to overrule an impeachment and conviction by Congress.

Section 2 Powers of the Executive, Cont'd

> **Clause 2.2 Advice and Consent, Treaties**
> He shall have Power, by and with the Advice and Consent of the Senate, to make Treaties, provided two thirds of the Senators present concur;

"to make Treaties"

Treaties require 2/3 approval from the Senate. Yet, the Court and the Senate have largely accepted Presidential control over foreign policy. Presidents interpret treaties under their power to govern foreign policy, and have even withdrawn treaties—without Senate advice and consent.

> **Clause 2.2a Appointments Clause**
> and he shall nominate, and by and with the Advice and Consent of the Senate, shall appoint Ambassadors, other public Ministers and Consuls, Judges of the supreme Court, and all other Officers of the United States, whose Appointments are not herein otherwise provided for, and which shall be established by Law:

"he shall nominate...Advice and Consent of the Senate"

The President selects whom he or she wishes to appoint. But the Senate must approve these choices.

Advice and Consent

In practice, Presidents consult with the Senate to gauge the acceptability of their choices. But the requirement that Presidents seek "Advice and Consent" applies only *after* they choose. Presidents need only gain the "consent" of the Senate. Any useful Senatorial "advice" is a bonus.

Section 2 Powers of the Executive, Cont'd

Clause 2.2b Inferior Officers

but the Congress may by Law vest the Appointment of such inferior Officers, as they think proper, in the President alone, in the Courts of Law, or in the Heads of Departments.

"vest the Appointment of...inferior Officers"

Congress (not the Senate alone) decides by law which federal officials and judges must be confirmed by Senate.

Clause 2.3 Recess Appointments

The President shall have Power to fill up all Vacancies that may happen during the Recess of the Senate, by granting Commissions which shall expire at the End of their next Session.

"Power to fill up all Vacancies"

Until recently Congress was out of session several months of the year. Thus, recess appointments were an important way to fill vacancies. More recently, Presidents have used this clause to slip controversial appointees into office. In response, Congress has resorted to "pro forma" sessions. Such actions are evidence of eroding "comity" or traditional courtesies and respect between the branches.

Section 3 Duties of the President

Clause 3.1 State of the Union Report

He shall from time to time give to the Congress Information of the State of the Union, and recommend to their Consideration such Measures as he shall judge necessary and expedient;

Section 3 Duties of the President, Cont'd

State of the Union

The President must report to Congress "from time to time." This report was originally delivered in written form to avoid seeming to violate the separation of powers. Woodrow Wilson began the modern tradition of presenting it in person.

Information of the State of the Union

What sort of information must the President give to Congress? The form of the State of the Union report is left undefined by the Constitution, but Congress has the power to pass specific reporting requirements into federal law as regards the Executive Departments.

"recommend to their Consideration such Measures"

By this clause presidents gain a formal role in lawmaking. Similar to the requirement that presidents report to Congress, this role is already implied by the President's role in signing or vetoing legislation, and in enforcing it.

Clause 3.1a Emergency Sessions of Congress

he may, on extraordinary Occasions, convene both Houses, or either of them, and in Case of Disagreement between them, with Respect to the Time of Adjournment, he may adjourn them to such Time as he shall think proper;

Convene and Adjourn Legislature

In times of emergency, the President may call the Senate and/or House into Special Session. No President has ever adjourned Congress under this power. See 1.5.4.

Clause 3.1b Receive Ambassadors

he shall receive Ambassadors and other public Ministers;

Section 3 Duties of the President, Cont'd

"receive Ambassadors"

Neither Congress nor the states have the power to negotiate directly with representatives of foreign powers. This power is reserved to the President. See Clause 2.2.2

> **Clause 3.1c Execute the Laws**
> he shall take Care that the Laws be faithfully executed,

"take Care that the Laws be faithfully executed"

If "the Laws" are solely those passed by Congress, this clause may limit more than it expands Executive power. But if it means he or she shall ensure lawfulness in general, then it expands Executive power. The "Take Care" clause has become a way for Presidents to take action to preserve domestic order in the absence of specific legislation.

> **Clause 3.1d Cont'd Commission Officers**
> and shall Commission all the Officers of the United States.

"Commission all the Officers of the United States"

A President can't do all the work of taking care that the laws be faithfully executed. Therefore, presidents appoint and commission officers to carry out these duties in accordance with the "Appointments Clause" (2.2.2a).

Section 4 Impeachment of Executive

> The President, Vice President and all civil Officers of
> the United States, shall be removed from Office on
> Impeachment for, and Conviction of, Treason, Bribery, or
> other high Crimes and Misdemeanors.

"Impeachment for, and Conviction of"

This is a two-step process. See Clause 1.2.6 and 1.3.6 for details
(see also 2.2.1a). Basically, the House of Representatives serves as a
Grand Jury. It makes the charge. The Senate serves as the court.

"Treason, Bribery... high Crimes and Misdemeanors"

The House of Representatives has the sole power to decide what
is an impeachable offence, and the Senate has the sole power
to decide whether it will convict based on that charge. Two
Presidents, Andrew Johnson after the Civil War, and William
Jefferson Clinton have been impeached. But the Senate has never
convicted a President of high crimes and misdemeanors. Richard
Milhous Nixon resigned before he could be impeached.

Article 3 Judiciary (Courts)

Much of the early wrangling over the meaning of the Constitution came from efforts of each branch to establish their power in relation to the others. This, for example, is why the Court's ruling in *Marbury v. Madison* (1803) is so important. In this case, the Court required the Executive to act according to its ruling, and the Executive did so. As head of a co-equal branch of government, President Jefferson might have insisted that his interpretations of the Constitution had as much weight as the Judiciary's. He didn't. *Marbury* was not a single, magic turning point; it was part of a historical process by which the Court increasingly established its role as final arbiter of the meaning of the Constitution. Today, the Court's Judicial Review powers are far more secure. Nevertheless, its role as such is not explicitly defined in the Constitution.

The mission of the Court has been to establish and protect its role. Lacking the legitimating institution of elections, it has had to build its place through persuasion and restraint.

For this reason, the Court adheres with almost religious fervor to decisions and reasoning of previous courts, that is, to precedents—the doctrine of "Stare Decisis." Think of the Court as semi-religious interpreters of the Constitution as scripture. Their power rests on their rectitude and their links to the long legal tradition. They live in constant danger of being ignored.

The adherence to precedents and legal custom helps to explain why the legal profession has clung to Latin phrases. English is a living language. The meaning of words and phrases take on additional connotations over time. Legal Latin, however, was used only in rarefied professional circles and its precision could be more easily guarded. (Less charitably: The more obscure the law, the greater its majesty, and the greater the job security of lawyers.)

Section 1 Organization of Courts

> **Clause 1.1 Organization of the Courts**
>
> The judicial Power of the United States, shall be vested in one supreme Court, and in such inferior Courts as the Congress may from time to time ordain and establish. The Judges, both of the supreme and inferior Courts, shall hold their Offices during good Behaviour, and shall, at stated Times, receive for their Services, a Compensation, which shall not be diminished during their Continuance in Office.

"and in such inferior Courts"

The Constitution creates a single court, the Supreme Court. Congress has created a three-tiered system with roughly 100 Federal District Courts, and various specialized courts for taxes, Veterans Appeals, International Trade, and others. Above them are 13 federal appeals courts. Above them is the Supreme Court.

Judicial Review

Nowhere, however does the Constitution spell out the principle of Judicial Review. The relationship of the Court to the other branches of government has been worked out in practice. The key case in which the Court insisted on its right to rule on the Constitutionality of the laws and actions of the other branches was *Marbury v. Madison* (1803).

Section 2 Scope of Supreme Court

Clause 2.1 Judicial Power (Arising)

The judicial Power shall extend to all Cases, in Law and Equity, arising under this Constitution, the Laws of the United States, and Treaties made, or which shall be made, under their Authority; to all Cases affecting Ambassadors, other public Ministers and Consuls; to all Cases of admiralty and maritime Jurisdiction; to Controversies to which the United States shall be a Party; to Controversies between two or more States; between a State and Citizens of another State; between Citizens of different States, between Citizens of the same State claiming Lands under Grants of different States, and between a State, or the Citizens thereof, and foreign States, Citizens or Subjects.

Arising Clause—"The judicial Power shall extend"

The Court rules only on disagreement regarding federal functions or statutes, and only between parties with standing to bring suit.

Comparative Note

The insistence that the Court only rule within specific cases is a particularly Anglo-American model. There are many models of justice in the world. Spanish and French judges, for example have far greater power to investigate on their own, and to initiate action.

"between a State and Citizens of another State"

The 11th Amendment limits the ability of citizens to sue states through the federal courts. The reason for this is to protect state sovereignty. The Court has created further limitations on the ability of Congress to create laws that allow citizens to sue their states. This is the reason that the main party with standing to bring suit against states is the Federal government.

Section 2 Scope of Supreme Court, Cont'd

> **Clause 2.2 Jurisdiction**
>
> In all Cases affecting Ambassadors, other public Ministers and Consuls, and those in which a State shall be Party, the supreme Court shall have original Jurisdiction. In all the other Cases before mentioned, the supreme Court shall have appellate Jurisdiction, both as to Law and Fact, with such Exceptions, and under such Regulations as the Congress shall make.

"original Jurisdiction"

Almost all cases come to the Court by appeal. Even in cases where the Constitution gives the Court the power to originate cases, it generally delegates that authority to specialized courts and reviews them on appeal.

> **Clause 2.3 Trial by Jury**
>
> The Trial of all Crimes, except in Cases of Impeachment, shall be by Jury; and such Trial shall be held in the State where the said Crimes shall have been committed; but when not committed within any State, the Trial shall be at such Place or Places as the Congress may by Law have directed.

"The Trial of all Crimes...shall be by Jury"

Trial by jury is a basic and ancient right in Anglo-American jurisprudence. See 6th Amendment.

Section 3 Treason

Clause 3.1 Defining Treason

Treason against the United States, shall consist only in levying War against them, or in adhering to their Enemies, giving them Aid and Comfort. No Person shall be convicted of Treason unless on the Testimony of two Witnesses to the same overt Act, or on Confession in open Court.

Treason

This clause answers the question: What is the difference between treason and disagreeing with the government? English law and monarchical governments in general had seen little division between disagreement with the Crown and treason. The Framers insisted that the term "treason" be defined narrowly and with a high standard of proof.

Clause 3.2 Limits on Punishment for Treason

The Congress shall have Power to declare the Punishment of Treason, but no Attainder of Treason shall work Corruption of Blood, or Forfeiture except during the Life of the Person attainted.

"Corruption of Blood, or Forfeiture"

Under English law, a person's family and heirs could be stripped of their property and status in perpetuity ("corruption of blood"). In this way the Constitution prohibits punishments from extending into future generations.

III. *Limitations on State Sovereignty*

Article 4 States

> **Clause 1 Full Faith and Credit**
> Full Faith and Credit shall be given in each State to the
> public Acts, Records, and Judicial Proceedings of every other
> State; And the Congress may by general Laws prescribe the
> Manner in which such Acts, Records and Proceedings shall
> be proved, and the Effect thereof.

"Full Faith and Credit"

Court records and judgments in one state must be honored in
another. So if you are sued and lose in one state, you cannot evade
judgment by moving to another, though the state may enforce the
judgment differently.

Section 2 Comity, or Mutual Respect

> **Clause 2.1 Privileges and Immunities**
> The Citizens of each State shall be entitled to all Privileges
> and Immunities of Citizens in the several States.

"Privileges and Immunities"

States may not discriminate against non-state citizens without good
reason. Good reasons to discriminate: to charge higher tuition
for state-supported education and higher hunting and fishing
licenses. New residents must be given the chance to "rebut the
presumption" that they are temporary residents (See *Vlandis v.
Kline* (1973)). Bad reason: to reserve jobs for local residents. See
14th Amendment for parallel language applying "privileges and
immunities" of US citizens to the states.

Section 2 Comity, or Mutual Respect, Cont'd

> ## Clause 2.2 Extradition Rules
> A Person charged in any State with Treason, Felony, or other Crime, who shall flee from Justice, and be found in another State, shall on Demand of the executive Authority of the State from which he fled, be delivered up, to be removed to the State having Jurisdiction of the Crime.

"Extradition Rules"

Persons who commit a crime in one state but have moved to another state must be handed over for trial.

> ## Clause 2.3 Fugitive Slave Clause
> No Person held to Service or Labour in one State, under the Laws thereof, escaping into another, shall, in Consequence of any Law or Regulation therein, be discharged from such Service or Labour, but shall be delivered up on Claim of the Party to whom such Service or Labour may be due.

"No Person held to Service or Labour"

"No Person" refers to slaves, as well as apprentices and indentured servants. Congress enforced the clause with the Fugitive Slave Act of 1793, though Northern states resisted it by requiring jury trials (which often nullified or refused to enforce the law) and refusing enforce it. See *Prigg v. Pennsylvania* (1842). The Compromise of 1850 included a new Fugitive Slave Act that eliminated juries, paid a bonus to slave catchers, required only a written assertion from the supposed former owner, and put any black person, former slave or not, at risk of being enslaved. This law, along with *Dred Scott* (1857) helped to convince Northerners that slavery was becoming less of a "peculiar institution" of the South and more of a national institution.

Section 3 Formation of New States

Clause. 3.1 Admissions Clause

New States may be admitted by the Congress into this Union; but no new State shall be formed or erected within the Jurisdiction of any other State; nor any State be formed by the Junction of two or more States, or Parts of States, without the Consent of the Legislatures of the States concerned as well as of the Congress.

"without the Consent of the Legislatures"

Congress can't split old states to create new states. Yet, in the Civil War, Virginia decided to secede and the region that became West Virginia decided to secede from Virginia. Vermont, Kentucky, Tennessee, and Maine were formed from state territories with the consent of their legislatures.

Northwest Ordinance of 1787

Congress under the Articles passed a law establishing the right of new states to enter the Union on an equal basis with existing states. The Framers wrote the New States clause with the Northwest Ordinance in mind.

Section 3 Formation of New States, Cont'd

Clause 3.2 Territories

The Congress shall have Power to dispose of and make all needful Rules and Regulations respecting the Territory or other Property belonging to the United States; and nothing in this Constitution shall be so construed as to Prejudice any Claims of the United States, or of any particular State.

Congress's Power in Territories of the United States

Congress has power to make laws and to rule over territories. The US has controlled several so-called "insular" or overseas territories such as Wake, Samoa, Guam, Puerto Rico, Virgin Islands, Northern Mariana Islands, and Guantanamo Bay Cuba. This designation also applies to military bases and embassies in sovereign nations, and to the Green Zone in Iraq. At different times, the US has controlled the Philippines, Haiti, and sundry other places. Congress classifies these territories as far as the extent to which American civil and other rights apply.

Section 4. Guaranty of Republican Government

The United States shall guarantee to every State in this Union a Republican Form of Government, and shall protect each of them against Invasion; and on Application of the Legislature, or of the Executive (when the Legislature cannot be convened) against domestic Violence.

"a Republican Form of Government"

The Court has largely ceded its role in deciding whether an individual state is properly maintaining a republican form of government. The short answer: Congress decides.

"The United States shall"

This is one of the cases in the Constitution where the term "The United States" refers to more of a single nation, rather than the plural suggested by "States."

IV. Ratification, Amending, and National Supremacy

Article 5 Amending Process

Article 5. Amending the Constitution

The Congress, whenever two thirds of both Houses shall deem it necessary, shall propose Amendments to this Constitution, or, on the Application of the Legislatures of two thirds of the several States, shall call a Convention for proposing Amendments, which, in either Case, shall be valid to all Intents and Purposes, as Part of this Constitution, when ratified by the Legislatures of three fourths of the several States, or by Conventions in three fourths thereof, as the one or the other Mode of Ratification may be proposed by the Congress; Provided that no Amendment which may be made prior to the Year One thousand eight hundred and eight shall in any Manner affect the first and fourth Clauses in the Ninth Section of the first Article; and that no State, without its Consent, shall be deprived of its equal Suffrage in the Senate.

"Application of the Legislatures of two thirds of the...States"

No amendments have ever been proposed by this method.

"when ratified by ... three fourths of the several states"

Only the 21st Amendment repealing Prohibition of alcohol was ratified by special conventions in the states.

Prohibiting Amendments to End Slavery Before 1808

Slave states insisted that their Constitutional right to own slaves not be amended before 1808. (See clauses 1.9.1 and 1.9.4). There is no prohibition on amendments regarding other aspects of slavery however, such as the Fugitive Slave Clause (4.2.3) or the Three Fifths Clause (1.2.3). Nevertheless, Ben Franklin was the lead signer on an abolitionist petition to the First Congress in 1789 that challenged legislators to abolish the slave trade despite these safeguards.

Article 6 National Supremacy

Clause 1. Continuity Clause

All Debts contracted and Engagements entered into, before the Adoption of this Constitution, shall be as valid against the United States under this Constitution, as under the Confederation.

Continuity of Obligations

This clause promises to respect obligations incurred under the previous national government. The clause reassured the nation's creditors and foreign governments.

Clause 2. Supremacy Clause

This Constitution, and the Laws of the United States which shall be made in Pursuance thereof; and all Treaties made, or which shall be made, under the Authority of the United States, shall be the supreme Law of the Land; and the Judges in every State shall be bound thereby, any Thing in the Constitution or Laws of any State to the Contrary notwithstanding.

"supreme Law of the Land"

This is another of the rare places where the Constitution speaks of the *nation* of the United States rather than a mere federation of states, united. Some critics feared this clause made states obsolete.

It didn't. But where was the line where national and state governments began and ended? The Court focused on this question in its first decades.

Clause 3. Oaths of Office

The Senators and Representatives before mentioned, and the Members of the several State Legislatures and all executive and judicial Officers, both of the United States and of the several States, shall be bound by Oath or Affirmation, to support this Constitution; but no religious Test shall ever be required as a Qualification to any Office or public Trust under the United States.

Allegiance of State Officials to National Constitution

State officials must declare their support for the national government. Since the Constitution includes the Supremacy Clause, this oath requires that state officials owe their allegiance to the national government. See the 14th Amendment Clause 3 that prohibits former officials of the Confederation from serving in an official capacity again.

Article 7 Ratification Process

Article 7 Ratification Process

The Ratification of the Conventions of nine States, shall be sufficient for the Establishment of this Constitution between the States so ratifying the Same.

"Conventions of nine States"

Amendment of the Articles required unanimous consent of all 13 states. The decision to require only 9 of the 13 in order to go into effect therefore essentially overturned the previous Constitution's provisions for amendment. In that sense, it overturned the previous form of government, and provided the means of creating a new one.

"between the States so ratifying the Same"

The Constitution by its own authority became law as of June 21st 1788 when New Hampshire ratified it by a 57-47 vote. By a similarly narrow vote, Virginia ratified it on June 25, 1788. But the states of New York (July 26), North Carolina (November 21, 1789), and Rhode Island (May 29, 1790) remained nominally outside the US until they ratified.

V. Amendments

Bill of Rights— First 10 Amendments

The first ten amendments are known as the "Bill of Rights." The Bill mostly lists individual rights the federal government is bound to respect. But it's more complicated than that.

- At first, it only limited the national government.
- The 14th Amendment (1868) seemed to promise transformation of the Bill into a list of rights owed all Americans by all levels of government, including states.
- This shift began early in the 1920s. It continues today.

Why did the Framers leave the Bill out?

The Constitution originally had no Bill of Rights. Opponents pointed to the missing Bill as evidence of a power grab. The Framers claimed that they had omitted the Bill because there was no need for one; the Federal government had no ability to do anything (such as abridge freedom of speech) that went unnamed. Moreover, to name a specific list of rights would be to suggest they were the *only* rights that the new national government was bound to respect. (The 9th Amendment addressed this issue.)

But proponents of the Constitution soon agreed that the first Congress would put forward such a Bill as a condition of passage. James Madison, originally an opponent of such a Bill, saw it as a chance to give the federal government some veto power over state laws. His amendment giving Congress this power failed to make the final list, however.

Bill of Rights as Limit on the Powers of Congress only:

In *Barron v. Baltimore* (1833) the Court formally ruled that the Bill applied to the national government, not the states.

Bill of Rights as Human Rights

Some observers before and after the Court established the precedent in *Barron v. Baltimore* nevertheless have insisted on seeing the rights in the Bill as basic guarantees of individual rights under natural and common law against all levels of government, be they national, state, or local.

That is, they saw the Bill as "Declaratory" of American rights under ancient tradition. Legally, they were wrong by 1833; the Court had explicitly ruled so. Rhetorically, the argument had power; not everyone read Supreme Court rulings.

Starting in the 20th century, the idea that the Bill of Rights listed basic human rights that all government agencies must respect has gained more legal power, and Americans routinely list the Constitution's Bill of Rights as a sacred, absolute, and inviolable list of human rights, almost a "Ten Commandments" for the government.

20th Century Rights Revolution

The project of protecting liberties became more complex as more Americans began to demand them. Rights were simpler when framers could largely envision them as the special possession of men who held a measure of social status and economic independence. The Framers tempered democracy with the unspoken assumption that a meritocracy of elites would rule, and that equality and rights would be handed out on a sliding scale.

But increasing numbers of Americans soon clamored for inclusion. Many white men made this claim at the dawn of the two-party system circa 1800, and exponentially so when mass political parties developed in the Jacksonian era (named after President Andrew

Jackson) of the 1830s. Immigrant groups such as Germans, Irish, and Italians in time claimed their due. After the Civil War, black male Americans claimed political rights with brief success (Women did at the time, too, but without even the temporary success of black men.). John Adams had predicted such a deluge with dismay early in the Revolution, warning that there would soon be no reason to exclude anyone at all from equality, including women and children.

The 20ᵗʰ century has seen Adams's prediction come true. There has been an explosion of groups claiming equal treatment under the law, including women. Children, too have gained additional civil rights such as to education and healthcare. The Civil Rights movement cracked open politics for African-Americans a hundred years after the Civil War. Hispanics and Indians made similar claims. That crack has proved wide enough for additional groups that heretofore had been kept to the margins, including homosexuals. The main groups whose equality the government seems able to evade today include political radicals, the very poor, new immigrants (especially illegal immigrants), and people, especially teenagers, who live in specific urban areas, whom the police have come to suspect as a class, and who have little political power.

Most defendants with court-appointed lawyers tend to settle for negotiated sentences rather than exercising their right for a trial by a jury of their peers. Wealth and celebrity bring defacto additional protections including increased procedural protections and energetic legal representation.

Transformative Impact of the 14ᵗʰ Amendment

At first, (1870s) the Court insisted that the 14ᵗʰ amendment had made little change in the meaning of the Bill. Late in the 19ᵗʰ Century, however, they decided that it *did* create a new national right for all Americans, but that it mostly protected *economic* liberty. In the "Laissez Faire" era (Roughly: 1880s – 1937), the Court prohibited almost *all* state economic regulations as infringements on "liberty of contract." (At the same time, it construed the "Commerce

Clause" power of Congress narrowly to prohibit most national economic regulation.) Only in 1938 did it begin to slowly rediscover the civil rights guarantees of the 14th Amendment. See discussion of 14th Amendment for more on Liberty of Contract and other issues mentioned here.

Progressive Challenge to Laissez Faire

Around 1900, some Americans began to argue that this new era of large-scale corporate power demanded government regulations to guarantee individual freedoms. Progressives argued that not only abuse of public governmental power (as envisioned by the Constitution) but also private accumulations of legal and monetary power could produce tyranny. Maximum individual liberty, Progressives insisted, required government limitations on private economic power. Especially in the case of individuals who were less able to freely negotiate for themselves, such as anthracite coal miners in an inherently dangerous, cartelized, company town industry, and women workers. (See President Theodore Roosevelt's intervention into the 1902 Anthracite Strike, as well as *Lochner v. New York* (1905) that the Progressives lost, and *Muller v. Oregon* (1908) where they gained a partial win.)

Civil Rights: A New Balance Point

The Court pulled back from protecting absolute property rights and from forbidding most economic legislation during the Great Depression. It indicated in a footnote that it would begin to protect civil rights for politically vulnerable groups (See footnote 4 in *US v. Carolene Products* (1938)).

As a result of the dicta (non-binding opinions of the court) expressed in *Carolene Products*, the Court slowly began to use the 14th Amendment as a new balance point for the entire Constitution. Civil rights became the focus of the Court's deliberations. Previously, Constitutional questions balanced less on notions of rights, and more on federal versus state powers, and the structure of government.

Incorporation of Bill of Rights through 14th Amendment

The process of defining civil liberties protected by the 14th Amendment in terms of the rights listed in the Bill is known as "incorporation." This means: The rights listed under the Bill should be considered basic liberties under the 14th Amendment (and therefore ought to be "incorporated" into its protections). Justice Hugo Black insisted that unless there was 100% incorporation, the Justices would simply be substituting their own judgment for that of state legislatures. Yet it has not been clear to a majority of justices that the 14th amendment ought to be so broad as to include such a blanket new limit on state sovereignty. Nor has the Court been willing to make such a massive change all at once. It has, more cautiously, practiced "selective incorporation," gradually ruling which rights ought to be incorporated as basic liberties, and which should not. Most recently, for example, the Court has been edging towards incorporating the 2nd Amendment right to bear arms.

Starting in *Chicago, Burlington & Quincy Railroad Co. v. City of Chicago* (1897) the Court effectively incorporated the 5th Amendment "takings clause" that prohibited the government from taking private property without due process and due compensation. It began to apply the "due process" clause of the 14th Amendment to state legal proceedings in *Twining v. New Jersey* (1908). It was not until *Gitlow v. New York* (1925) however that the Court began to explicitly list liberties so fundamental that they would henceforth be incorporated through the 14th Amendment's due process clause. *Gitlow* incorporated 1st Amendment freedom of speech and press.

See specific Amendments for their incorporation status.

1st Amendment—Speech, Press, Assembly, Religion, Petition

The first ten Amendments (Bill of Rights) were ratified effective December 15, 1791.

> Congress shall make no law respecting an establishment of religion, or prohibiting the free exercise thereof; or abridging the freedom of speech, or of the press, or the right of the people peaceably to assemble, and to petition the Government for a redress of grievances.

1st Amendment Outline

1. Establishment Clause
   a. Separation of Church and State
   b. Lemon Test
2. Freedom of Speech
   a. Flag Burning
   b. Commercial Speech
   c. Political Speech
   d. Obscenity and Pornography
3. Freedom of the Press
   a. Peter Zenger—Pre-Constitutional Precedent
   b. Pentagon Papers
   c. Libel and Parody
4. Peaceably to Assemble
5. Petition the Government
6. Incorporation of the 1st Amendment
7. Student Free Speech

1. Establishment Clause

"no law respecting an establishment of religion"

Controversy was caused by the 1st Amendment's incorporation of the Establishment Clause through the 14th Amendment in *Everson v. Board of Education* (1947) (See below under "Incorporation of 1st Amendment"). The Establishment Clause was hardly an issue for much of our history. But states and municipalities had long regulated religion and morality. This new rule thus undermined existing connections between church and state.

For example, it made legally-required Christmas pageants and recital of the Lord's Prayer more difficult to sustain as neutral exercises of government power. Previously, parents and children of non-Protestant faiths had simply adapted to these facts of life, "hmmm hmming" key words to religious songs, enrolling in private schools, or (in at least one high school drama club) insisting that all actors in a state-mandated school Christmas Pageant be Jewish "for reasons of historical accuracy."

a. Separation of Church and State

The original reasons for separating church and state came from a desire to keep the church free from government corruption. This was Roger Williams's reason for attacking Puritan theocracy in the 1630s. Today, religious activists seem more interested in using religion to purify government—to bring back old community limits on moral behavior.

b. Lemon Test

In *Lemon v. Kurtzman* (1971) the Court created three tests to decide whether state actions violated the Establishment Clause. Laws must: Have a non-religious purpose, tend neither to help nor to hurt religion, and not excessively entangle government and religion. If a law did any of these three things, it was unconstitutional. See *Kitzmiller v. Dover Area School District* (2005).

The problem of Court rulings on the Establishment Clause came from the doctrine that Court rulings apply universally, coherently, and consistently. Once the Court decided to rule on separation of church and state it stepped into the bewildering complexity and variety of local rules and religions, as well as the long-accepted practice of putting religious mottos on coins and in oaths. Once it decided that government had to be kept out of the business of policing religion, it came into conflict with already-established public practices entwined with religion.

"Free Exercise Thereof"

The Court applied "strict scrutiny" test developed for Civil Rights cases against government regulation of religious practices starting with *Sherbert v. Verner* (1963). In this test, the government had to show a "compelling interest" in regulating a religious practice. In the 1980s and 1990s, the Court authorized more government regulations. In *City of Boerne v. Flores* (1997), the Court ruled that Boerne had the right to impose zoning ordinances on a church without violating the free exercise clause. That is, Boerne did not have to show a "compelling interest" because its zoning ordinances were neutral in regard to religion.

2. Freedom of Speech

The first-ever ruling on freedom of speech came in *Schenck v. US* (1919) and in the context of World War I. Eugene Debs went to prison for encouraging resistance to the draft in World War I (*Debs v. US* (1919)). Thousands were convicted of criticizing the WWI effort or obstructing the draft. (Prior to 1919, guarantees of free speech were largely dormant. The Alien and Sedition Acts of 1798, passed in order to prevent criticism of Federalists, were allowed to expire in 1801.)

Most people remember *Schenk* for Justice Oliver Wendell Holmes, Jr.'s comparison of anti-war activism to yelling fire in a crowded theater. He actually likened it to *falsely* yelling fire in a crowded theater. Holmes himself quickly abandoned this metaphor, so much more vivid than helpful. (What, he was asked, if the theater actually *was* on fire?) Yet, even without Holmes's support, his original reasoning helped establish broad limits on free speech among a majority of Justices. (In a dissent later in the year (*Abrams v. US* (1919)), Holmes sought to narrow the definition of "Clear and present danger" more to acts than speech.)

Nevertheless, in *Gitlow v. New York* (1925) the Court confirmed its original view of the "clear and present danger" test. At the same time, it broke new ground, stating that freedom of speech that was *not* a clear and present danger would now be considered a core liberty under the 14th Amendment (see "6. Incorporation of the 1st Amendment"). The Court expanded protection of speech that advocated violence and resistance to the law in *Yates v. US* (1957). In *Brandenburg v. Ohio* (1969), it established a new, stricter test for when speech became illegal: "imminent, lawless action." (This result overturned the conviction of an Ohio KKK leader for threats against blacks and Jews.)

a. Flag Burning

In *Texas v. Johnson* (1989) the Court ruled that burning the flag was a legitimate exercise of free speech.

b. Commercial Speech

Prior to 1976, rules prohibited lawyers and doctors from advertising. So-called "ambulance chasers," (personal injury lawyers) had to actually *chase* the ambulances to sign up injured clients. They couldn't just put billboards up along the likely route to the hospital or air TV commercials.

Nor were drug companies allowed to advertise prescription drugs. Now they can. See *Bates v. State Bar of Arizona* (1977), *Greater New Orleans Broadcasting Association v. US* (1999) and *Thompson v. Western States Medical Center* (2002).

c. Political Speech

The Court uses "strict scrutiny" to judge the Constitutionality of state or federal laws limiting political speech. It has been particularly suspicious of laws that limit spending on political campaigns. The Court has permitted campaign finance laws that require disclosure of contributions, and that limit individual contributions to campaigns (*Buckley v. Valeo* (1976)). But it insisted that individual persons be able to spend as much of their own funds as they wish on their own campaigns. Most recently, the court struck down limits on the right of corporations to pay for commercials or videos on political themes during federal campaigns. See *Citizens United v. Federal Election Commission* (2010).

d. Obscenity and Pornography

Outside of child pornography, the Court has steadily made it harder to censor speech. The "Roth Rule" from *Roth v. US* (1957) outlawed pornography that violated community norms. But this assumed a community. Pornography also had to come into the community in order to be obscene (not simply be stashed in a drawer). (*Stanley v. Georgia* (1969)) Neither Court nor Congress has found a consistent test to define adult pornography without appeal to community standards. Justice Potter Stewart's declaration that "I know it when I see it." (*Jacobellis v. Ohio* (1964)) did not suggest a wish to review potential subjects himself. Rather, it indicated the difficulty of stating a consistent rule. His, after all, was simply a one-person version of the Roth Rule.

3. Freedom of the Press

Main issues include "prior restraint" (prevention of publication), the press's right of access to government meetings, and post-publication prosecution for libel or breach of national security. (In today's age of Internet-based publication, the distinction between freedom of speech and freedom of the press has blurred.)

a. Peter Zenger—Pre-Constitutional Precedent

In this 1735 case, the jury found Peter Zenger Not Guilty of seditious libel even though his newspaper had indeed illegally criticized the government. The truth, the jury argued, was a sufficient defense against a charge of libel. This precedent precedes the U.S., and therefore it precedes the 1st. Nevertheless, it served as part of American legal custom. Note, too that the jury nullified the law, ignoring instructions from the judge. (See Bushell's case, 1670 under 6th Amendment below.)

b. Pentagon Papers

In *New York Times Co. v. US* (1971), the "Pentagon Papers" case, the US attempted to get a court order preventing prior publication of secret reports on national security grounds (as if the contents were equivalent to shipping schedules during wartime). The court refused to so order.

c. Libel and Parody

In the early 1960s, as the press began to write about resistance to Civil Rights, some Southern public officials responded to the criticism with libel suits against Northern newspapers. The Court issued a ruling in *New York Times Co. v. Sullivan* (1964) that raised a high bar for such suits. They had to show more than factual errors to prove libel, the Court ruled. For a public individual to sue the press for libel, he or she would have to show that the press knowingly acted with "actual malice," or with deliberate recklessness or maliciousness. *Hustler Magazine v. Fallwell* (1988) protected parody and satire. Note: Parody and satire are protected even if the subject doesn't find it funny.

4. Peaceably to Assemble

The right to assemble in support of such awful political causes as racism and anti-Semitism is protected along with the right of people to assemble in support of such good causes as tolerance. (See *Village of Skokie v. National Socialist Party of America* (1977)). The 1st Amendment protects minority positions, even awful ones. Since the 1960s, the Court has largely refused to define, or to recognize adjectives such as "awful" or "good" as related to political causes or speech.

5. Petition the Government

The government has less scope to regulate political speech in traditionally public areas such as parks. But it may make content-neutral regulations as to the Time, Place, and Manner (TPM) of protests. Recently, police and Secret Service have more aggressively used "Free Speech Zones" to remove protesters from places near politically charged events such as presidential speeches. This became more widespread after disruption of the World Trade Association meeting in 1999, and during George W. Bush's presidency.

6. Incorporation of the 1st Amendment

The Court incorporated the freedom of the press to publish without prior restraint by the states as guaranteed by the 14th in *Near v. Minnesota* (1931). State and federal governments were allowed prior restraint only in cases of urgent national security (publishing shipping schedules during wartime) or obscenity. Individuals damaged by false and malicious publications could sue for damages after the fact, but they could not prevent publication.

7. Student Free Speech

Students gained free speech during the 1960s era of Civil Rights and anti-Vietnam War protest. See *Tinker v. Des Moines...* (1969). This, however, was for symbolic speech (black armbands). More recently, public school students have been punished for advocating drug use, or other causes argued to be disruptive to education or student privacy. See *Bethel School District No. 403 v. Fraser* (1986), *Morse v. Frederick* (2007), and *Hazelwood School District v Kuhlmeier* (1988).

2nd Amendment— Right to Keep and Bear Arms

> A well regulated Militia, being necessary to the security of a free State, the right of the people to keep and bear Arms, shall not be infringed.

"well regulated"

Think, "well organized." Think, "well-connected to a legitimate, established political entity," (such as a town or community).

"Militia"

A "militia" or "training band" in colonial America was as much a duty as a right. All law-abiding male citizens in a town were *required* to maintain functioning firearms, to attend training days, and to serve in the militia. If they failed to do so they were subject to penalties. They elected officers and served with neighbors. Militia defended each town. In the Revolution, militia fought with the Continental army, and defended against British Loyalists.

The militia was not quite the equivalent of today's National Guard (The Guard is closer to the sort of standing army that the militia was supposed to be a check against). It's perhaps closer to a Volunteer Fire Department today in the mix of informal voluntarism and formal community and government support.

"the people"

The "militia" and "people" were largely synonymous in this context. They were not "the individuals" but the same "people" in "We the people" who begin the Preamble.

"keep and bear Arms"

The right – and obligation – of individuals to own (keep) weapons, and to carry (bear) them in their militia.

"shall not be infringed"

The right to keep and bear military-style arms has long been infringed by community standards and state law. (The 2nd originally limited *national* law only.) Infringement by federal law is more recent. The National Firearms Act was passed in 1934, largely in response to the rise of organized crime during Prohibition, and largely in order to regulate the supposed weapons of organized crime: sawed off shotguns, machine guns, grenades, and the like. Using the Commerce Clause as its authority, the NFA imposed a prohibitive tax on the interstate sale or transfer of such weapons. In a limited ruling in *US v. Miller* (1939), the Court upheld the law. The law has been amended and reaffirmed by Congress several times since 1939.

Impact of Civil War and 14th Amendment

Akhil Reed Amar's book, *The Bill of Rights*, captures a sense in which the emphasis of the 2nd Amendment shifted between 1789 and 1868. He writes: "In Reconstruction a new vision was aborning: when guns were outlawed, only the Klan would have guns." (266) The importance of the 2nd Amendment for Northern reformers had become more about individual defense against "private violence and the lapses of local government" rather than on collective local defense against a tyrannical national army.

US v. Miller (1939)

The Court upheld the right of the national government to regulate interstate commerce of firearms. The court's reasoning was in part based on the supposed inappropriateness of a sawed-off shotgun, the type of weapon that was seized in this case, for militia use. Although the Court has recently begun to veer from some of the logic of the *Miller* ruling as regards interpretation of the Militia clause, it has let stand the NFA's effective limits on more destructive, military-style weapons – such as sawed off shotguns. One might well argue that the militia clause ought to *particularly* prevent infringement of the right to own military-style weapons! But discouraging private ownership of machine guns, howitzers, missiles of various kinds, modern fighter jets, grenades and atomic bombs—have been commonly accepted as reasonable limits on 2nd Amendment rights. *Miller* limited the right to bear arms to those small arms that a citizen (and therefore a potential militia member) might commonly be expected to keep at home (Acceptable weapons include rifles, standard shotguns, and handguns.)

Presser v. Illinois (1886)

Allowed states to forbid private militias. The right to bear arms, the Court argued, was an individual right. The right to regulate militias was a state function. The 2nd limited the national government not the states.

Dred Scott v. Sandford (1857)

Suggested that *if* the slave Dred Scott were free and white, he would be protected by the 2nd Amendment in his individual right to bear arms.

US v. Cruikshank (1875)

Prevented the national government from guaranteeing the right of individuals – in this case black freedmen who had armed themselves to defend against the Ku Klux Klan – to bear arms. This was solely a state function. (A state function, it should be noted, that Southern states had no intention of fulfilling. The KKK would now deprive black citizens of their rights without fear of interference from the national government.)

Today's 2nd Amendment

Today's 2nd Amendment has focused on the right of individuals to possess firearms for *private* use. That is, for target-shooting, hunting, and individual self-defense. The 2nd Amendment's guarantee of a collective right to organize a well-regulated militia in resistance against a potentially tyrannical government has faded somewhat in the Court's reasoning. This notion nevertheless retains something of a hold in informal constitutionalism, if not in current legal precedent.

Individual Right to Keep Arms

In *DC v. Heller* (2008), the Court overruled a Washington, DC law banning all handguns and requiring that other weapons be stored in a manner that would prevent their rapid use for self-defense. A total ban on handguns (In this federally-controlled city) was ruled unconstitutional under the 2nd Amendment. Most recently, in *McDonald v. Chicago* (2010) the Court seems to have incorporated the right to bear arms in self-defense.

Note: The Court has upheld laws limiting gun ownership for the mentally incompetent and for felons.

3rd Amendment— Quartering Troops

> No Soldier shall, in time of peace be quartered in any house, without the consent of the Owner, nor in time of war, but in a manner to be prescribed by law.

This largely obsolete amendment referred to a grievance listed in the Declaration of Independence. It may be seen, in concert with the 2nd Amendment as a guard against standing armies. It's also cited in scattered cases, and in finding a right to privacy in *Griswold v. Connecticut* (1965).

4th Amendment— Unreasonable Search and Seizure

> The right of the people to be secure in their persons, houses, papers, and effects, against unreasonable searches and seizures, shall not be violated, and no Warrants shall issue, but upon probable cause, supported by Oath or affirmation, and particularly describing the place to be searched, and the persons or things to be seized.

This amendment limits when government officials may come into your house, harass you anywhere else, frisk, poke around, arrest, trespass, or otherwise violate your wish to be left alone. It has two main parts.

The first part has come to mean: The government may violate this right as long as it does so in a manner and for reasons that the Court sees as "reasonable."

The second part explains what it means by "reasonable": A representative of the Judicial branch may authorize a representative of the Executive branch to search and/or seize specific places and/or specific persons for specific reasons stated under oath. Those reasons must show "probable cause" to believe criminal activity is taking place. Searches and/or seizures made without a warrant are generally assumed to be unreasonable.

91

4th Amendment— Warrantless Searches/Seizures

Warrantless Searches/Seizures

Can the government arrest, question, search, seize, or detain you without getting a warrant? Probably. Rules on the 4th Amendment are complex and technical. In sum: the Court generally privileges the government's duty to keep society secure over your 4th Amendment rights.

History: A man's house is his castle (not).

The most famous declaration of the English freedom from arbitrary searches is William Pitt's declaration in Parliament, 1763. "The poorest man may in his cottage, bid defiance to all the forces of the Crown. It may be frail, its roof may shake; the wind may blow through it; the storm may enter; the rain may enter; but the King of England may not enter; all his forces dares not cross the threshold of the ruined tenement." Pitt lost. The intrusive tax law passed.

But American lawyers across the Atlantic heard him. The Revolution was born in resistance to the right of British tax collectors to enter and seize property without specific warrants, claimed John Adams. Adams and others were particularly angry about Navigation Acts that gave British customs officials almost unlimited power to search property. Adams was in the audience when American lawyer James Otis echoed Pitt's "Castle" speech in the "Writs of Assistance" or "Paxton's Case" (1761). British customs officials, Otis insisted were forbidden to search private property without a specific warrant. It should be noted that like Pitt, Otis *lost* his case. Any search authorized by the king was accepted as legitimate under English courts.

Otis and Pitt based their reasoning on the Common Law argument regarding scope of the Magna Carta of 1215. The 4th Amendment was a direct response to this dispute. It's fascinating, complex, and worth your time. See Leonard Levy *Origin of Bill of Rights*.

Unreasonable Searches and Seizures

Abolitionists looked in vain to the 4th Amendment's guarantee of freedom to void the Fugitive Slave Act. Though they claimed that it ought to protect free blacks from warrantless seizure under the Fugitive Slave Act, the Court decided in *Jones v. Van Zandt* (1847) that this was an essentially political question for state and federal authorities to battle out on their own.

Incorporation

In *Mapp v. Ohio* (1961), the Court incorporated parts of the 4th Amendment as one of the 14th Amendment's "due process" liberties. It thereby began to develop and to apply uniform rules across the entire nation.

Exclusionary Rule

What if the FBI ignored the 4th Amendment, broke down your door, and found evidence of a crime? From *Weeks v. US* (1914) to *US v. Leon* (1984), the Court required that such evidence be automatically excluded from your trial. They reasoned that without such a rule, federal officers would have little incentive to respect 4th Amendment limitations. Between 1914 and 1961, the Exclusionary Rule remained applicable only to federal cases, and to states that chose to adopt it.

Chipping Away at the Exclusionary Rule

Despite the importance of this rule in forcing police to professionalize, it galled prosecutors and judges, seeming to protect criminal activity more than a basic respect for privacy. The Court increasingly weakened this aspect of the 4th Amendment even as it insisted that the right to privacy was a basic liberty. (See the desire to reject *Weeks* in the majority opinion in *Wolf v. Colorado* (1949)).

Objective Good Faith

The Court has relaxed its strict Exclusionary Rule to the extent that it has been able to argue that so doing will not encourage police illegality. It has decided that if police find evidence of wrongdoing even with a flawed warrant it is admissible. *US v. Leon* (1984)

Prohibition Era. Automobiles.

In the Prohibition era (1920-1933), the federal government expanded its law enforcement efforts. In particular, federal agents began tapping telephones and searching cars (two activities probably not envisioned by the Founders). The Court refused to rule eavesdropping a violation of the 4th Amendment, even when it involved wiretapping or other electronically-enhanced efforts. *Olmstead v. US* (1928). It reversed itself in *Katz v. US* (1967). In *Carroll v. US* (1925) the Court ruled that 4th Amendment prohibitions may be relaxed when searching automobiles for alcohol. The Court has continued to give the police greater latitude to search automobiles.

5th Amendment— Due Process, Property

> No person shall be held to answer for a capital, or otherwise infamous crime, unless on a presentment or indictment of a Grand Jury, except in cases arising in the land or naval forces, or in the Militia, when in actual service in time of War or public danger; nor shall any person be subject for the same offense to be twice put in jeopardy of life or limb, nor shall be compelled in any criminal case to be a witness against himself, nor be deprived of life, liberty, or property, without due process of law; nor shall private property be taken for public use without just compensation.

This amendment stops the federal government from prosecuting individuals for arbitrary or political reasons, and from doing so in an unfair manner. The limitations on the government's power to prosecute have been incorporated by the due process clause of the 14th Amendment. Thus they are applicable in state and local law as well.

"No person"

These rights apply to all *persons* under the jurisdiction of the United States, not only citizens.

"Grand Jury"

The government cannot simply order that a person be put to trial. A group of ordinary citizens must agree that the trial is warranted. This ancient right was originally conceived as a guarantee against arbitrary arrest and trial. With the modern tools of corps of investigators and prosecuting attorneys, and the tactical leakage of damning information to the press, the Grand Jury has become less of a guarantee against arbitrary prosecution and more of a means of gathering evidence before trial. Grand Juries, because they are not prosecuting crimes, have far more leeway for compelling testimony.

Grand Jury Incorporation

The Court has not seen the 5th Amendment guarantee of a Grand Jury as fundamental under the 14th Amendment. Therefore, it is not binding on the states. About ½ of all states require grand juries for serious crimes already.

"twice in jeopardy" (Double Jeopardy)

Criminal trials are awful, damaging ordeals for defendants. The government must be prevented from using repeated trials themselves as punishment. In actual practice, the right to not be charged twice for the same crime is complicated by technical questions, mostly revolving around three questions: When does a trial truly begin? What is the same crime? What is the same punishment?

"compelled... to be a witness against himself

No one can be forced to incriminate himself. This hard-won right is rooted deep in British and American history. Here is the logic: The government, with its monopoly on coercion, must build the case on its own. It cannot demand that you build a case against yourself.

When Is a Confession Truly Voluntary?

The Court largely stayed out of the business of settling such matters until recently. After all, its job was to set rules of interpretation, not to peek over the shoulders of police detectives in grubby interrogation rooms. It left details of law enforcement to communities. Only the most brutal of abuses compelled the Court to intervene. In *Brown v. Mississippi* (1936) three black men were publicly tortured until they confessed, and the torture was part of the official evidence of the case. This case takes us back to the origins of the right against forced self-confessions in ancient British precedent, when the King's prosecutors compelled confessions or pleas through torture.

Miranda Rules

Once they weighed in on what constituted a voluntary versus a compelled confession they found themselves on slippery ground. The Court took 30 years from *Brown* in 1936 to the so-called

Miranda rules (from the name of the case *Miranda v. Arizona* (1966)).

Miranda rules insisted on specific, legalistic grounds on which criminal defendants could be questioned. First, defendants had to be informed of their rights. Second, once they asked for their 6th amendment right to counsel, *all* questioning had to stop. The so-easily caricatured ("You have the right to *shut up!*") ritual of *Mirandizing* suspects responded to a world in which the police at times abused their awesome power to detain, isolate and intimidate, particularly against vulnerable groups with limited access to political power. See: "Third degree," in reference to widespread use of abusive means to extract confessions.

Limiting Miranda

The first *Miranda* era excluded any self-incriminatory testimony that seemed to have been compelled *in any way whatsoever*. The Court seemed to assume confessions in the context of an arrest were suspect. Proof of a compelled confession could "taint" any subsequent prosecution and require the entire case to be thrown out no matter how strong the rest of the evidence.

Without directly overruling *Miranda*, the Court has steadily moved away from its requirements. In *Arizona v. Fulminante* (1991) the Court ruled that a coerced confession could be thrown out without tainting the rest of the evidence in the case. The Court has allowed police more leeway as they have seemed to become more restrained, professional guardians of law—and as the egregious abuses of earlier eras fade from memory.

"due process of law"

The original meaning of this term focuses on fair procedures. The government is only granted the massive power of depriving a person life liberty and property if it follows fair and consistent rules tested by long usage.

Substantive Due Process

The Court first used this reasoning in regards to the right of slaveholders to their human property in the infamous *Dred Scott v. Sandford* decision (1857). The substance of the right to property, the Court argued, was so important that there existed no due process by which Congress could take such property (slaves) from their owners. Therefore, it ruled, Congressional limits on ownership of slaves were unconstitutional. Congress wrote the 14th Amendment in part to overrule this decision.

See the 14th Amendment below for discussion of the Court's Gilded Age (1870-1900) revival of substantive due process. Here again the Court deemed property rights to be so important as to prohibit states from regulating almost any aspect of economic activities.

Abolitionist Argument

Abolitionists argued that since slaves were persons they could not be deprived of life or liberty under this clause. If there were any such thing as substantive due process, they argued, it should free all slaves.

"nor shall private property be taken..." *Takings Clause*

Given the various interpretations of the Court, this clause might as well read: "The government has the right to use your property as long as it can connect it to a reasonable public purpose. It probably has to reimburse you." See *Kelo v. City of New London* (2005). Post *Kelo*, most states have passed laws preventing such takings in future.

"except... in the land or naval forces, or in the Militia..."

Military personnel do not receive precisely the same guarantees as private citizens. Nevertheless, Congress's rules for the military (authorized by clause 1.8.14 above) must conform to due process requirements, and to 8th Amendment limitations on cruel and unusual punishment.

6th Amendment— Speedy Trial, Counsel

> In all criminal prosecutions, the accused shall enjoy the right to a speedy and public trial, by an impartial jury of the State and district wherein the crime shall have been committed; which district shall have been previously ascertained by law, and to be informed of the nature and cause of the accusation; to be confronted with the witnesses against him; to have compulsory process for obtaining witnesses in his favor, and to have the assistance of counsel for his defence.

The 6th Amendment names rights so fundamental that they have all been incorporated through the due process clause of the 14th Amendment and therefore apply to the states.

"accused shall enjoy the right to a speedy and public trial"

When is a trial not "speedy"? When a judge decides that it's been unduly delayed for no good reason, that the defendant complained about the delay within a reasonable amount of time, and that the delay has been substantial and had a negative impact on the defendant's case. Unless these conditions apply, the 6th Amendment will see the case as "speedy." As a defendant, be forewarned that it may not *feel* speedy, and despite the wording, you will not enjoy it. If, however, your right to a speedy trial has been violated the judge must dismiss the case.

"public trial"

Courts cannot try and convict defendants in secret proceedings shielded from public scrutiny. Fairness requires openness. Nevertheless, trials can be shielded from public view to protect defendants or for various reasons such as national security. They may not be closed more than absolutely necessary.

"impartial jury"

The Founding generation saw juries as a vital check on government power. Today we see juries almost entirely in their role in deciding guilt or innocence. But in the 18th century, especially in pre-democratic Britain, the right and obligation of jury duty was more akin to the right and obligation to vote. Juries made inherently political decisions about what sorts of persons and crimes were worth punishing.

Jury: Nullification

Jurors cannot be punished for their decisions. Colonial American juries often acquitted smugglers and others who ran afoul of English law. Juries have acquitted defendants because they decided the crime was justified. Prior to and during the Civil Rights movement, all-white juries refused to convict white defendants who committed crimes against non-whites. The right of jurors to reject the strict letter of the law without punishment was established in English Common Law in 1670. Jurors found William Penn (of Pennsylvania fame) innocent of illegal preaching despite instructions to the contrary from the judge in the case. (Bushell's case, 1670). In this important sense, juries reach back to an ancient, pre-democratic purpose of giving commoners a limit on the law. See also Peter Zenger 1735 libel case under 1st Amendment.

When do Defendants Have the Right to a Jury Trial?

Trials for crimes punishable by 6 months or more in prison entitle the defendant to a jury trial. Federal juries must consist of 12 jurors, and their decisions must be unanimous. State juries may consist of 6 jurors. State juries of 12 may convict by a supermajority. State juries of 6 may only convict by unanimous vote

"have the assistance of counsel for his defence"

The right to counsel (a lawyer), whether the defendant could afford it or not became incorporated in *Gideon v. Wainright* (1963). Prior to that case, the Court had occasionally ruled that the right to counsel only applied in cases where the defendant was unusually disabled in his or her defense, possibly because of being illiterate.

7ᵗʰ Amendment—Jury Trial

> In Suits at common law, where the value in controversy shall exceed twenty dollars, the right of trial by jury shall be preserved, and no fact tried by a jury shall be otherwise reexamined in any Court of the United States, than according to the rules of the common law.

This amendment has not been incorporated as a basic liberty that states must accept.

"In Suits at common law"

In any civil suit filed at the federal level, defendants have the right to insist on a jury, or to waive that right. The jury may have 12 persons (standard) or 6.

"and no fact tried by a jury"

On appeal, a judge can set aside a verdict, or reduce an award as excessive. But the judge may not challenge the jury's findings of fact. Appellate judges may only examine points of law and due process.

8th Amendment— Cruel and Unusual Punishment

> Excessive bail shall not be required, nor excessive fines imposed, nor cruel and unusual punishments inflicted.

"Excessive bail shall not be required"

The system allowing defendants to put up bail to guarantee their presence at trial is the product of long tradition. The previous alternative was to detain defendants until trial. The Court has spent little effort on defining "excessive bail." Until 1966, judges were required to give bail for defendants unless they were deemed a flight risk, or if they were accused of a capital crime. In 1984, a new federal law allowed judges to deny bail if defendants were deemed dangerous to the community, and expanded the list of serious crimes that justified denial of bail.

"nor cruel and unusual punishments inflicted"

Incorporated through the 14th Amendment's due process clause in *Robinson v. California* (1962). From the late 1960s through the early 1980s, the Court made the death penalty more difficult for the states to impose. Since 1987, the Court has steadily made it easier, and has declined to rule punishments to be cruel or unusual, or to decide whether punishments are proportionate to the crime.

9ᵗʰ Amendment—
This List of Rights Is Not Complete

> The enumeration in the Constitution of certain rights shall not be construed to deny or disparage others retained by the people.

Natural Rights

The Framers were concerned that listing rights in the Constitution and Bill of Rights might convey the notion that *only* these rights were to be protected. Americans saw themselves as endowed with a wide variety of rights, not all of which were mentioned in the Constitution or Bill. The rights listed in the Constitution and Bill, and therefore denied to the federal government should not be considered an exhaustive and complete list.

Right to Privacy

In 1965, the Court decided that one of the natural rights included in the 9ᵗʰ Amendment included the right to privacy. Using the metaphor of a "penumbra," (a sort of shadow) the 1ˢᵗ, 2ⁿᵈ, 3ʳᵈ, 4ᵗʰ, 5ᵗʰ, and 9ᵗʰ amendments put together, it argued, implied a right to privacy. (*Griswold v. Connecticut* (1965)). Although the Court has largely abandoned the reasoning that tied the right to privacy to the 9ᵗʰ Amendment, several cases have expanded on the right to privacy based on the due process and equal protection clauses of the 14ᵗʰ Amendment (Most famously, *Roe v. Wade* (1973)). See below.

Part of the point of the 9ᵗʰ Amendment is to remind us that the American written Constitution has always existed in the prior context of unwritten assumptions regarding the privileges due human beings by virtue of their humanity. That is, the Constitution was written, existed, and exists, in the context of a traditional constitutionalism.

10th Amendment—
Powers Retained by States, People

> The powers not delegated to the United States by the
> Constitution, nor prohibited by it to the States, are reserved
> to the States respectively, or to the people.

Put simply, the Bill did not list *all* the limitations on Congress. It
did not, by implication add any powers to the national government
that it had somehow failed to prohibit.

Expressly (not)

This amendment was sometimes understood by states rights advocates as if it read "The powers not *expressly* delegated to Congress
shall be reserved to the states and the people." During the Gilded
Age and Progressive era (1870s-1920s) when the Court was fight-
ing a rearguard battle to stop Congressional economic regulation, it
agreed with this interpretation. It outlawed the federal Child Labor
Act (1916) for example, as interference with states. (See *Hammer v.
Dagenheart* (1918)). (Note: The Articles of Confederation included
this term in Clause 2, but the Framers deliberately omitted it from
the 10th Amendment.

Decline of the 10th: "truism"

In *US v. Darby* (1941) the Court began to treat the 10th as a truism,
as if it did no more than to state the obvious.

Federalist Revival

Starting in *National League of Cities v. Usery* (1976) the Court
began to more carefully define rights of the states that, though not
listed in the Bill or elsewhere in the Constitution were not to be
infringed on by the Congress. The Court has increasingly argued
that in our system of dual federalism, federal regulations cannot be
forced on the states. See *Garcia v. San Antonio Metropolitan Transit
Authority* (1985), *New York v. US* (1992), *Printz v. US* (1997), *US
v. Morrison* (2000).

11th Amendment— States Cannot be Sued

Proposed March 4, 1794. Ratified February 7, 1795.

The Judicial power of the United States shall not be construed to extend to any suit in law or equity, commenced or prosecuted against one of the United States by Citizens of another State, or by Citizens or Subjects of any Foreign State.

Sovereign Immunity

This amendment overturned the Court's decision in *Chisolm v. Georgia* (1793). In this case, the Court allowed citizens of South Carolina to sue Georgia. Its importance is in how it underlined the sovereign immunity of states, and thereby reinforced the system of dual federalism. See *Hans v. Louisiana* (1890) and *Alden v. Maine* (1999).

12th Amendment— Presidential Elections

Proposed December 9, 1803. Ratified June 15, 1804.

The Electors shall meet in their respective states, and vote by ballot for President and Vice President, one of whom, at least, shall not be an inhabitant of the same state with themselves; they shall name in their ballots the person voted for as President, and in distinct ballots the person voted for as Vice President, and they shall make distinct lists of all persons voted for as President, and of all persons voted for as Vice President, and of the number of votes for each, which lists they shall sign and certify, and transmit sealed to the seat of the government of the United States, directed to the President of the Senate;

The President of the Senate shall, in the presence of the Senate and House of Representatives, open all the certificates and the votes shall then be counted; The person having the greatest number of votes for President, shall be the President, if such number be a majority of the whole number of Electors appointed, and if no person have such majority, then from the persons having the highest numbers not exceeding three on the list of those voted for as President, the House of Representatives shall choose immediately, by ballot, the President. But in choosing the President, the votes shall be taken by states, the representation from each state having one vote; a quorum for this purpose shall consist of a member or members from two-thirds of the states, and a majority of all the states shall be necessary to a choice. And if the House of Representatives shall not choose a President whenever the right of choice shall devolve upon them, before the fourth day of March next following, then the Vice President shall act as President, as in the case of the death or other constitutional disability of the President

The person having the greatest number of votes as Vice President, shall be the Vice President, if such number be a majority of the whole number of Electors appointed, and if no person have a majority, then from the two highest numbers on the list, the Senate shall choose the Vice President; a quorum for the purpose shall consist of two thirds of the whole number of Senators, and a majority of the whole number shall be necessary to a choice. But no person constitutionally ineligible to the office of President shall be eligible to that of Vice President of the United States.

Function and History

This amendment replaces clause 2.1.3 because of a problem unforeseen by the Framers: Political Parties. The original plan: the person with the highest majority of electoral votes became President. The person with the second highest number of votes became Vice President. (See 2.1.3 on the Electoral college for more details.)

The new plan: Instead of naming their two top candidates, each elector names a candidate for President and a candidate for Vice President.

Problem solved: In the old system, President and Vice President might well be from rival parties (This happened with John Adams and Thomas Jefferson in 1796.) or party-line Electoral votes would result in a tie between President and Vice President.

13th Amendment—Slavery Ended

Proposed, January 31, 1865. Ratified December 6, 1865.

Section 1. Neither slavery nor involuntary servitude, except as a punishment for crime whereof the party shall have been duly convicted, shall exist within the United States, or any place subject to their jurisdiction.

Section 2. Congress shall have power to enforce this article by appropriate legislation.

First Reconstruction Amendment

The first 12 amendments either limited the power of the Federal Government or clarified the Constitution. The 13th Amendment ended the right of humans to own each other, and *added* to the power of the Federal Government.

Black Codes

Immediately after the Civil War, states of the former Confederacy began to pass so-called "Black Codes" to keep former slaves as close to their former condition as possible. These replaced the "Slave Codes."

Expansive Reading

Republicans at first thought that the 13th Amendment would be the only post-Civil War change to the Constitution. Once slavery was abolished, former slaves would gain civil and political rights. According to the "expansive reading" of the 13th Amendment, Congress's power to enforce an end to slavery also gave Congress power to enforce an end to the "badges and incidents" of slavery such as "Black Codes," and other forms of racial discrimination.

Civil Rights Act of 1866

Congress confirmed its expansive reading of the 13th Amendment by passing the Civil Rights Act of 1866 over President Andrew Johnson's veto. This Act declared all persons born in the US to be citizens of the US, and required that they receive the equal protection of the law in all states. At the same time, Congress reauthorized the Bureau of Freedman Affairs that intervened on the side of former slaves. In both cases, Congress empowered federal officials to enforce national law.

13th Amendment Revived, 1968

Over 100 years after its first passage, the Court overturned its earlier narrower rulings on the 13th Amendment and confirmed the more expansive reading. The Civil Rights Act of 1866 prohibited housing discrimination starting in 1968. (*Jones v. Alfred H. Mayer Co.* (1968))

14th Amendment—Civil Rights

> Proposed June 13, 1866. Ratified July 9, 1868.
>
> Section 1. All persons born or naturalized in the United States and subject to the jurisdiction thereof, are citizens of the United States and of the State wherein they reside. No State shall make or enforce any law which shall abridge the privileges or immunities of citizens of the United States; nor shall any State deprive any person of life, liberty, or property, without due process of law; nor deny to any person within its jurisdiction the equal protection of the laws.

Prior to the Civil War, the Court focused on balancing state and national power. The 14th attempted to limit local and state capacity for tyranny as well as the national government. The 14th therefore transformed American Constitutionalism.

   I. Why an amendment? (Two Crises)
  II. Chronology of 14th Amendment
 III. Structure of 14th Amendment
     Section 1. States are prohibited from abridging
       1. National Citizenship; National Liberties
       2. Privileges and immunities
       3. Due Process
       4. Equal protection of the laws
     Section 2. Penalty for Restricting the Vote
     Section 3. Disqualification for Former Confederates
     Section 4. Repudiation of Confederate War Debt
     Section 5. Congress shall have power to enforce

1. Why an amendment? (Two Crises)

Radical Republicans used the Amendment to address two crises, detailed in the following two sections.

    a) To stop extra votes for the South.
    b) To enforce racial equality before the law.

a) To stop extra votes for the South.

After the Civil War, the South was due to reap a windfall of voting power from freed slaves. The 14th was supposed to stop former slaveholders from controlling that power.

The 3/5 clause (1.2.3) counted state population for the number of House members and Electoral College votes given to each state. Each slave counted as 3/5 of a person. Each free person counted as one person. Every former slave thus added to the power of the South by 2/5 of a person. Radical Republicans feared (rightly) that Southern whites would keep the electoral bonus gained by the end of slavery but prevent black former slaves from wielding political power.

b) To enforce racial equality before the law.

Between 1865 and 1868, former Confederates maintained white supremacy through "Black Codes" and often-lethal violence against black leaders. Black Codes required non-whites to work only in farm jobs and for year-long contracts. As in slave times, blacks had to get permission to leave the plantation, or be arrested for vagrancy. In short, the Black Codes were an attempt to return former slaves as closely as possible to the condition of slavery. The 14th was a second attempt to overturn the Black Codes after the 13th failed to do so.

14th Amendment Chronology

1870s: Zombie 14th Amendment

The goals of the 14th amendment suffered from too much support in 1873 and too little support starting in 1876. In the *Slaughterhouse Cases* (1873) Justice Samuel Miller loved the goals of the 14th too much. He was a Radical Republican committed to Reconstructing the South on racially egalitarian grounds. When New Orleans whites demanded that the Court overturn new laws passed by the state's multiracial legislature, Miller saw it for what it was: an effort to revive white supremacy. A medical doctor himself, Miller wished to support Louisiana's efforts to regulate slaughterhouses. (New Orleans butchers had previously slaughtered and dumped carcasses upstream of the city's water supply.)

Miller's opinion largely returned the guarantee of civil rights to the states, as it had been before the 14th. This made sense at the time: Miller wished to support the multiracial Reconstruction government of Louisiana.

But Miller's gamble failed. Northerners began to abandon Southern blacks in the mid-1870s (See Tilden-Hayes Compromise of 1877 that exchanged Republican control of the Presidency with an end to Reconstruction.) and white supremacists began to take back control of state governments throughout the South. For if the Union forces were victorious on the battlefield in 1865, after 1876 the Ku Klux Klan and other groups, often led by former Confederate soldiers reimposed white supremacy in Southern state governments.

Black leaders and their white supporters were terrorized, humiliated, killed, and exiled. (It is worth noting that blacks and their allies resisted such terrorism in the 1870s and 1880s, and that when activism *was* possible, they and their allies built on the living, if closely-held community memory of early Reconstruction era triumphs. That community memory came alive in the Civil Rights movement.)

1880s–1890s: Reanimation

Property Rights

After 1873, the Court moved with increasing decisiveness to create a national standard of citizenship under the 14th – for individual property rights. Since the *Slaughterhouse Cases*, dissenting Justice Stephen Field had seen in the 14th Amendment a way to defend the rights of property against state governments. The states, he thought, were too tempted to side with farm and labor activists against railroads, grain silo companies, and the new large-scale manufacturing and mining businesses.

The Court invalidated a state law in *Allgeyar v. Louisiana* (1897) under the due process clause. The Court had been moving in this direction for some years, but had been slow to act definitively. In *Munn v. Illinois* (1877) and *Railroad Commission Cases* (1886) the Court declared that states could regulate businesses when those businesses engaged in enterprises "affected with a public interest", but the Court would judge whether such regulation was reasonable. Starting with *Allgeyar*, and solidifying in *Lochner v. New York* (1905), the Court declared almost all economic regulations to be unreasonable.

In this line of cases, the Court protected "liberty of contract" of individual persons against government regulation. (In *Santa Clara County v. Southern Pacific* (1886) the Court had declared corporations to be legal persons.)

States were not permitted to pass laws regulating hours or conditions of labor unless such laws were state "police power" necessary to protect the health and welfare of their citizens. Legislators had to show a suspicious Court that their laws were not intended to protect workers, or to support unions. They had to be passed solely to protect the health of the public. (Or to protect particularly at-risk worker such as coal miners. See *Holden v. Hardy* (1898)).

Women's Health Exception

In *Muller v. Oregon* (1908), future Court Justice Louis D. Brandeis argued that excessive hours for women would undermine the health of the people of Oregon. He intended his argument to be an "opening wedge" to insist that too many hours was unhealthy for men, too. (In *Bunting v. Oregon* (1917) the Court upheld such regulations for men as well.) In *Adkins v. Children's Hospital* (1923) it refused to apply the argument for *Muller* to minimum wages.

1937: Reasonable Economic Regulation Permitted

New Deal Constitution: "Switch in time that saved nine."

With Justice Owen Roberts as the swing vote between Progressives and the conservative "Four Horsemen," the Court had been taking small steps towards overturning its anti-state-regulations stance in *Lochner*. (See *Nebbia v. New York* (1934) and *Home Building & Loan Association v. Blaisdell* (1934) for more Court deference to state laws.) But Roberts joined a pro-*Lochner* decision just two years later (in *Morehead v. Tipaldo* (1936) overturning a state minimum wage law). Yet in *West Coast Hotel v. Parrish* (1937), he joined the majority to overrule the Liberty of Contract precedent of the Allgeyer/*Lochner* era. The Court began to permit "reasonable" state economic regulations.

People at the time called Justice Roberts's vote in favor of the New Deal the "switch in time that saved nine" because it seemed to come in response to President Franklin D. Roosevelt's threat to pack the Court with more justices. It's more complex than that (Roberts changed his vote *before* FDR issued his threat, and the

Court had toyed with small changes in 1934.), but the impact of FDR's landslide victory in 1936, the real threat that he would indeed pack the Court, and public sentiment that portrayed the Court as a roadblock to progress undoubtedly played a role as well.

The Court overturned its old interpretation of the Commerce Clause. It now permitted most economic regulations (1.8.3).

1938: Rediscovery of Civil Rights

Strict Scrutiny of Racial Laws

One year after *West Coast Hotel*, in *Carolene Products* (1938) the Court tentatively rediscovered Civil Rights. It would now allow almost all *economic* regulations. But it would more carefully scrutinize laws that violated "a specific prohibition of the Constitution, such as that of the first ten amendments," or if they undermined the freedoms of "discrete and insular minorities" (especially if such minorities had limited access to political power). The Court buried its new determination in footnote number 4 of the decision. Economic regulations would need pass only minimal scrutiny as having a "rational basis," while those laws that violated the Bill would face "strict scrutiny." In *Korematsu v US* (1944) strict scrutiny failed to protect over 100,000 Japanese Americans from internment.

1954: Attack on Segregation

Civil Rights Era—Brown v. Board of Education (1954)

Before *Brown v. Board of Education* (consistent with its "separate but equal" ruling in *Plessy v. Ferguson* (1896) and *Yick Wo v. Hopkins* (1886)), the Court agreed that legally segregated facilities had to be equal in *fact* as well as in formal assumption. Eventually, the Court would rule in *Brown* that "separate is inherently unequal."

This directly overturned *Plessy* in regard to education, but as important, overturned the logic of *Plessy* that generally accepted segregation laws as long as they preserved a formal equality. In *Missouri ex rel. Gaines v. Canada* (1938) the Court ruled that when a state provides education for whites, it must provide an equal education non-whites. (*Canada* referred to S.W. Canada, registrar of the Univ. of Missouri, not the nation of Canada.) In *Sweatt v. Painter* (1950) the NAACP lawyers focused more on whether a new, separate law school for non-whites could ever truly be "equal." It was a deeply persuasive argument to the law school graduates on the Court, proud as they were of their alma maters. *Sweat*, then, began to press the question of whether separate could *ever* be equal.

The Court ruled in *Brown* that "separate educational faciities are inherently unequal." This May 17, 1954 ruling created "massive resistance" in Southern states that still practiced legal segregation. It would eventually also undermine the long tradition of neighbor-hood schools in the North, segregated by residential patterns and redlining, and lead to similar Northern scenes of massive resistance.

Brown therefore began the avalanche of rulings that struck down nearly all government-sponsored racial discrimination against blacks. (See also Commerce Clause 1.8.3 rulings such as *Heart of Atlanta Motel v. US* (1964) above that built on the logic of *Brown*, but used the broad grant of economic power gained through the New Deal Commerce Clause to empower Congress to outlaw discrimination in public facilities such as hotels, motels, and restaurants.)

1970–Present: Affirmative Action and Backlash

The broader point of the rulings in *Brown v. Board*, *Hearts of Atlanta* and other civil rights era cases was to end all discrimination against black citizens. As Martin Luther King put this point, it made good on a promissory note signed by the Founding Fathers in the Declaration of Independence and renewed in the Gettysburg Address (and 13th, 14th, and 15th amendments). Yet proponents of equality argued that the affects of discrimination – hundreds of years of systematically preventing blacks from accessing equal education, good jobs, and political power meant that equality before the laws meant entrenched, structural inequality. As a post-Civil War white planter argued, freed slaves gained "nothing but freedom." That is, they gained nothing but freedom to live in a segregated, white supremacist society without individual savings or the savings of generations, education, equal protection of the law, credit, or political power.

The Court has increasingly taken a dim view of affirmative action, seeing it as simply another form of race-based law. The first key case was *Regents of the University of California v. Bakke* (1978). Only if race was considered in order to rectify past wrongs, and was only one of several criteria, individually evaluated, could affirmative action stand. The court has nibbled at this logic in a series of cases, but allowed it to stand. *Grutter v. Bollinger* (2003).

1973: Abortion

Until January, 1973, abortion was a state matter, outlawed in some states and permitted in others. The debate focused on public health of women and "back alley" abortions. Since *Roe v. Wade* (1973), the debate has shifted to one of competing absolute rights – the right of the fetus to life v. the right of the woman to control her body, and precisely where one set of rights ends and the other begins. Some argue that life begins at the moment of conception, some when it can survive outside the womb, some at points in-between. After *Roe* was handed down in January 1973, abortion became a 14th Amendment liberty under the "due process" clause, and based also on the *Griswold v. Connecticut* (1965) case outlining a right to privacy. As abortion has become a matter of right and religion, room for compromise has disappeared.

In *Roe*, the Court ruled that a woman's right to make decisions regarding her own health was a paramount liberty. At the same time, the government also had a right to protect life before birth. In the first trimester, states were not permitted to regulate her choice of whether or not to abort the fetus. In the second trimester the states could regulate this choice in ways related to the health of the mother. In the third trimester, the states could regulate abortions. In all of these judgments, however, medical judgment regarding the health of the mother had to remain primary.

Several states have passed laws attempting to limit access to abortions by imposing waiting periods, requiring doctors to counsel patients on the decision, and outlawing some forms of abortion. The Court has consistently agreed that a woman's right to end her pregnancy is one that may be abridged only at the margins. A small majority of justices has accepted *Roe* as settled law whether they agree with it or not. A solid minority has consistently argued that it should be overturned. A woman's control over whether or not to abort, they argue, should be removed from its status as a paramount 14th Amendment liberty, and returned to the states.

Planned Parenthood v. Casey (1992) reaffirmed the core reasoning of Roe, but allowed state regulations to start outweighing the wishes of the mother at the point of viability according to current medical technology. It also lessened *Roe's* high level of Court scrutiny of such laws. *Gonzales v. Carhart* (2007) permitted a federal statute outlawing a form of 3rd trimester abortion procedure.

2000: Equal Protection and the Vote

Bush v. Gore (2000) ended the recount in the Florida Presidential vote on the grounds that ballots were being evaluated according to different criteria in different places. Therefore, the Court argued, it violated equal protection.

14th Amendment— Structure—Section 1

Structure of 14th Amendment

Section 1. States are prohibited from abridging

1. National Citizenship; National Liberties
2. Privileges and Immunities
3. Due Process
4. Equal protection Under the Law.

Section 1. States are prohibited from abridging

1. National Citizenship; National Liberties

"All persons...are citizens"

In the *Dred Scott v. Sanford* (1857) decision, Justice Roger B. Taney (pronounced "Tawney") argued that blacks were automatically excluded from citizenship. This section of the 14th directly overturned Taney's ruling. It created a right of national citizenship. It overruled the presumption that people became national citizens only to the extent that they became state citizens.

But in the Court's *Slaughterhouse* (1873) opinion, Justice Miller sought to maintain the balance between national and federal power as it had existed before the Civil War. He read these first two sentences of the 14th as if they simply restated the existence of state and national citizenship, not as a new standard of national citizenship.

2. Privileges and Immunities

This seems to have been a way of referring generally to Constitutional guaranties of liberty, whether stated in the text, in the Bill, or in Common Law. (See 4.2.1 for parallel language requiring that the "privileges and immunities" of citizens of one state be respected in the others.) The term came from English common law, social contract ideas of John Locke, and *Blackstone's Commentaries*.

"Immunities" were natural rights that the people did not need to give up to the government in order for it to function. "Privileges" were rights (personal security, liberty, and property) that the government agreed to protect in return for being granted its power by the people. An expansive definition can be found in *Corfield v. Coryell* (1823) "Protection by the government; the enjoyment of life and liberty, with the right to acquire and possess property of every kind, and to pursue and obtain happiness and safety."

But the Court rejected the above expansive nature definition of the amendment in *Slaughterhouse*. According to the Court, the clause protected only very basic rights such as the right to travel. (This narrow definition of the term is why attempts to "incorporate" basic liberties through the 14th had to rely on the "Due Process" clause. See below.)

3. Due Process

"No State shall...deprive any person..."

Controversy regarding this phrase centers on the terms "liberty" and "due process," repeated from the 5th Amendment. The Due Process clause required that states respect due process for *all* persons, whether citizens or not.

Substantive Due Process

See 5th Amendment above for discussion of this issue.

After *Slaughterhouse* (1873) narrowed Privileges and Immunities, the doctrine of "Substantive Due Process" came to stand for those liberties so basic that states were forbidden from abridging them. See "Liberty of Contract," for example.

4. Equal Protection Under the Law

After the Civil War, Southern state Black Codes singled out former slaves and free blacks for special punishment and regulation. This section of the amendment responded directly to the Black Codes. Because of the generous wording of this term, it would eventually be applied to an increasing number of classifications (men, women, immigrants, ethnicities, homosexuals, ages, religions).

Equal Protection—Formal Equality Versus Equality in Fact

Strauder v. West Virginia (1880) made it illegal for states to explicitly exclude blacks from jury duty. States achieved this goal through less-direct means. *Yick Wo v. Hopkins* (1886) stated that formal equality in drafting a statute could not excuse inequality in fact.

Plessy v. Ferguson (1896) ruled that state segregation laws were reasonable as long as they were universal and equal in their scope. They had to equally prohibit different races from mixing, simply adding the force of law to established community custom. They could not, for example, prohibit blacks from mixing with whites, but allow whites to mix with blacks. If black people chose to see such laws as discriminatory, the Court stated, that was their own choice. In practice, "separate but equal" protected only separateness, not equality. *Brown v. Board* (1954) would later (much later) argue that segregation by law automatically implied a judgment of inferiority, and thus, contrary to *Plessy*, segregation laws were inherently unequal.

Equal Protection and Access to Public Spaces

The Civil Rights Act of 1875 required equal access to public places such as trains, taverns and theaters. It relied on the Equal Protection clause for its power. But the Court struck down this section of the law, arguing that "equal protection" referred only to equality before the law, not to equal access. *Civil Rights Cases* (1883). See *Plessy v. Ferguson* (1896).

Equal Protection and State Versus Private Action

The Court ruled that the 14th protected blacks solely if state governments did the discriminating and explicitly said so. Victims of lynch mobs, KKK members, and other non-state actors could not turn to the national government for protection. They had to rely upon white supremacist state governments. Nor could the national government step in to protect US citizens if state governments refused to protect them. See *US v. Harris* (1882) ("Ku Klux Klan Cases"), and *Civil Rights Cases* (1883), in which it overruled the Civil Rights Act of 1875 for similar reasons.

Equal Protection and the Vote

In *Reynolds v. Sims* (1964) the Court made its "one man one vote" ruling that districts had to be of similar population. Beyond population, equal protection forces the Court to unpack complex local issues and motives. It is ill-equipped for this task. The Court has generally seen gerrymandering as a political matter when motivated by party. What of districts set up to elect a person of a single race? Illegal. *Shaw v. Reno* (1993). But a district set up to elect a Democrat (acceptable) might also be racial, since most blacks vote Democrat. *Hunt v. Cromartie* (1999). The current rule regarding gerrymandering is unclear.

Bush v. Gore (2000) relied on equal protection to stop the count of ballots in the presidential election of that year.

Marriage

States have refused to accept some out-of-state marriages because they violated state laws on polygamy, age, or same-sex marriage. States may not limit marriages in ways that violate the 14th. *Loving v. Virginia* (1967) overturned Virginia's 1924 anti-mixed-race law. (So yes, if the Court someday rules that state anti-same-sex marriage laws violate the 14th, it may overturn them.)

Section 2 Penalty for Restricting the Vote

> Representatives shall be apportioned among the several States according to their respective numbers, counting the whole number of persons in each State, excluding Indians not taxed. But when the right to vote at any election for the choice of electors for President and Vice President of the United States, Representatives in Congress, the Executive and Judicial officers of a State, or the members of the Legislature thereof, is denied to any of the male inhabitants of such State, being twenty-one years of age, and citizens of the United States, or in any way abridged, except for participation in rebellion, or other crime, the basis of representation therein shall be reduced in the proportion which the number of such male citizens shall bear to the whole number of male citizens twenty-one years of age in such State.

Males

The abolitionist and women's suffrage movement was closely interlocked. Radical Republicans were well aware that they were selling women down the river here. This is the first time the term "male" appears in the Constitution.

Irony

This clause should have lowered electoral votes and Congressional representation to the extent that a state deprived eligible voters from voting. It was never exercised. Even after Southern states almost entirely disenfranchised blacks, Congress never put this clause into action.

Section 3 Disqualification for Former Confederates

> No person shall be a Senator or Representative in Congress, or elector of President and Vice President, or hold any office, civil or military, under the United States, or under any State, who, having previously taken an oath, as a member of Congress, or as an officer of the United States, or as a member of any State legislature, or as an executive or judicial officer of any State, to support the Constitution of the United States, shall have engaged in insurrection or rebellion against the same, or given aid or comfort to the enemies thereof. But Congress may by a vote of two-thirds of each House, remove such disability.

This was an attempt to prevent former Confederate leaders from taking their old places in Congress, Senate, and state governments. It didn't last long. By 1872, Congress applied it only to Congressmen and Senators who served during secession. By 1898 it repealed the penalty entirely.

Section 4 Repudiation of Confederate Debt

> The validity of the public debt of the United States, authorized by law, including debts incurred for payment of pensions and bounties for services in suppressing insurrection or rebellion, shall not be questioned. But neither the United States nor any State shall assume or pay any debt or obligation incurred in aid of insurrection or rebellion against the United States, or any claim for the loss or emancipation of any slave; but all such debts, obligations and claims shall be held illegal and void.

Debt issued in the name of the Confederacy or Confederate states was not to be repaid. For the complexities of this section, including whether Confederate states ever legally left the Union, see *Texas v. White* (1869). This section also erased any ambiguity on whether former slave owners would be paid for lost human property. They would not.

Section 5 Power of Enforcement

> The Congress shall have power to enforce, by appropriate legislation, the provisions of this article.

By 1883, the Court had narrowed this clause almost out of existence. See *Civil Rights Cases* (1883), for example.

15th Amendment—
Right to Vote for Black Males

> Proposed February 26, 1869. Ratified February 3, 1870.
>
> Section 1. The right of citizens of the United States to vote shall not be denied or abridged by the United States or by any State on account of race, color, or previous condition of servitude.
>
> Section 2. The Congress shall have power to enforce this article by appropriate legislation.

Lack of a Federal Bureaucracy

The national government was poorly equipped to enforce regulations in this era. The 15th therefore relied on the federal judiciary. The Court was a slender reed, however. Despite Court rulings, it took development of a federal bureaucracy, a Civil Rights movement, the Voting Rights Act of 1965, a resurgent Court and the 24th Amendment outlawing poll taxes to guarantee non-whites the vote.

Why Wasn't the Right to Vote Part of the 14th Amendment?

Without black votes, advocates didn't have the power in Congress. But Radical Reconstruction under the 14th Amendment gave enough blacks and Northern supporters the vote for enough time, and with enough support to pass the 15th Amendment.

Impact?

Once Reconstruction slowed to a halt in 1876, white supremacist state governments used legal tricks short of overt declaration to deny blacks their right to vote. Combined with private primaries for the Democratic Party, one party (Democratic) rule, and Ku Klux Klan terrorism if all else failed, Southern states made the 15th a dead letter.

Legal Tricks

One trick was the "Grandfather Clause." All citizens were required to pass a literacy test unless they or a relative had been able to vote before Reconstruction. Illiterate white citizens were therefore able to vote. Local election supervisors invariably disqualified blacks, literate or not. The Court invalidated literacy tests in *Guinn v. US* (1915). This first case involving lawyers from the National Association for the Advancement of Colored People (NAACP) was something of a toothless victory. Neither the Court, nor any other federal or state officials took action to enforce it. Other tricks included poll taxes, segregated political parties, racial gerrymandering, and locally administered tests that supposedly measured Constitutional knowledge, but really measured the administrator's judgment of skin color.

Voting Rights Act of 1965

This act targeted those states with an established prior record of voter discrimination based on race. From an initial focus on ensuring that all qualified voters be able to vote without discrimination, the Court has since turned its attention towards the acceptable makeup of voting districts and the question of whether states can establish a track record of non-discrimination sufficient to be free from federal government regulation. See *South Carolina v. Katzenbach* (1966) for the acceptable reach of federal laws. See *Allen v. State Board of Election* (1969).

16th Amendment—Income Taxes

Proposed July 12, 1909. Ratified February 3, 1913

The Congress shall have power to lay and collect taxes on incomes, from whatever source derived, without apportionment among the several States, and without regard to any census or enumeration.

Income Taxes

This amendment avoided a direct confrontation between Congress and the Court. It responded to the Court's ruling in *Pollock v. Farmers' Loan & Trust Company* (1895). The Court ruled taxes on any income from property or land were direct taxes, and thus had to be apportioned according to a state's level of federal representation (1.2.3).

Direct Tax

Prior to *Pollock*, the Court defined direct taxes narrowly, therefore broadening Congress's taxing powers. From 1862 to 1872 (when the law expired) the US had an income tax. In 1881, the Court ruled that the Civil War era income tax was "indirect." Because it was not a direct tax, it was not covered by clause 1.2.3 or 1.9.4 (*Springer v. US* [1881]).

Income Tax Ruled Unconstitutional

When Congress passed an income tax in 1894, then, there was little concern regarding its Constitutional status. The tax was the product of a widespread Progressive, Populist, Labor coalition. But the Court struck it down. The Court's decision was broadly seen as a last-ditch defense in a battle between economic class interests. The Court struck down any tax on income from property as a direct tax. (It supposedly authorized income taxes on wages, but since it forbade taxes on any wages derived from property, few wages could really be taxed.)

17th Amendment—
Election of Senators by Voters

Proposed May 13, 1912. Ratified April 8, 1913.

Section 1. The Senate of the United States shall be composed of two Senators from each State, elected by the people thereof, for six years; and each Senator shall have one vote. The electors in each State shall have the qualifications requisite for electors of the most numerous branch of the State legislatures.

Section 2. When vacancies happen in the representation of any State in the Senate, the executive authority of such State shall issue writs of election to fill such vacancies: Provided, That the legislature of any State may empower the executive thereof to make temporary appointments until the people fill the vacancies by election as the legislature may direct.

Section 3. This amendment shall not be so construed as to affect the election or term of any Senator chosen before it becomes valid as part of the Constitution.

Popular Election of Senators

Senators were originally selected by state legislatures. (See Clause 1.3.1) One of the markers that shifted the Gilded Age to the Progressive Age was the rising chorus against corporate influence in legislatures. The Senate became a symbol of corrupt government.

This amendment solved several problems with the Senate, as it had come to evolve over the years. By 1911, when the measure passed both House and Senate, over half the states, led by Oregon had set up ways to achieve popular election of Senators. Essentially, they passed laws requiring the legislature to select as Senator the winner of a statewide election. The 17th supplied a formal way for states to fill vacancies mid-term if their legislatures gave state governors that power. It also prevented states from substantially narrowing the qualifications for Senator.

White Supremacy

A main obstacle to turning popular election of Senators from a state-level reform to a formal Constitutional Amendment was the Southern Democratic whites-only primary system. Since Reconstruction, one way Southern Democrats had exerted whites-only control over their political system was by confining all political decision-making to Democratic primaries. The few African Americans who managed to vote without being lynched could do so only in the Republican primaries, or in the popular elections. To elect Senators by popular vote, Southerner politicians feared, might allow black voters to have a say in the selection of Senators. This fear (unfortunately) proved unfounded.

Filling Vacancies by State Executive

In case of a vacancy, this amendment allows state governors to name a person to serve out the term (if the state legislature so permits them).

18th Amendment— Liquor Outlawed

Proposed December 18, 1917. Ratified January 29, 1919. Repealed by 21st Amendment, December 5, 1933.

Section 1. After one year from the ratification of this article the manufacture, sale, or transportation of intoxicating liquors within, the importation thereof into, or the exportation thereof from the United States and all territory subject to the jurisdiction thereof for beverage purposes is hereby prohibited.

Section 2. The Congress and the several States shall have concurrent power to enforce this article by appropriate legislation.

Section 3. This article shall be inoperative unless it shall have been ratified as an amendment to the Constitution by the legislatures of the several States, as provided in the Constitution, within seven years from the date of the submission hereof to the States by the Congress.]

Revenge of the South and West

This third of four Progressive amendments (16th, 17th, 18th, and 19th) was the first led by the Southern and Western strain of Progressive reform. Starting in 1909 and peaking in 1917, 24 Southern and Western states passed bans on alcohol. Such bans had little impact on the mint julep supply for the Kentucky Derby, but made purchase of alcohol difficult for poor whites and blacks in the South, and for immigrants in the West. A large number of rural towns and states all over the country followed suit. The national ban on alcohol followed this state-by-state experiment.

(Even after repeal, many states, counties, and towns stayed dry, or created laws to make purchase of alcohol difficult, or at least annoying.)

Unintended Consequences of Prohibition

An amendment intended to make Americans better people pro-moted lawlessness. Urban and Northern Americans responded with the largest civil disobedience campaign in American history. Before long, bars in New York City stopped hiding themselves. Organized crime expanded to take advantage of the opportunity. Federal surveillance of ordinary Americans, already given a hard push in the Palmer Raids by US Attorney General A. Mitchell Palmer against Socialists and in attacking anti-war sentiments during World War I, gained another boost for its battles against alcohol. In response to organized crime the Court vastly expanded the scope of federal law-enforcement and surveillance.

Death of the Public House

The Framers often Assembled at taverns to talk politics and recruit soldiers. All American Marines learn the story of the Corps's founding at Tun Tavern in Philadelphia. Indeed, the story of the militias and the Revolution is so linked to taverns and alcohol that the Court *might* have banned state laws that unreasonably infringed on the right of citizens to drink. The Court might have seen the 1st Amendment right to assemble, combined with the 2nd Amendment right to bear arms as implying a right to bend elbows in the kinds of taverns where Americans originally recruited fighters and planned rebellion. (It didn't. To my knowledge, the Court never, ever even considered this argument. Still, this informal right is preserved in custom. Disobeying the letter of the law, some bartenders illegally accept military ID as proof of sufficient age whether the bearer is 21 or not.)

19ᵗʰ Amendment— Women Gain the Vote

19ᵗʰ Amendment

Proposed June 4, 1919. Ratified August 18, 1920.

The right of citizens of the United States to vote shall not be denied or abridged by the United States or by any State on account of sex. Congress shall have power to enforce this article by appropriate legislation.

The Flip Side of Prohibition?

In 1920, Northern and Western states combined to give women the vote. By this time, most non-southern states permitted women to vote. The main issue for the South was (as with direct election of Senators—See 16ᵗʰ Amendment) white supremacy in electoral politics. A new federal voting right posed the threat that the national government might begin to regulate voting rights. If so, it might begin to enforce the rights of *black* women and men to vote, as required in the 15ᵗʰ Amendment. They needn't have worried. The federal government did not require Southern states to grant the vote to black women.

20th Amendment— Details about Dates of Office

Proposed March 3, 1932. Ratified January 23, 1933.

(Six sections listed below.)

Section 1. The terms of the President and Vice President shall end at noon on the 20th day of January, and the terms of Senators and Representatives at noon on the 3d day of January, of the years in which such terms would have ended if this article had not been ratified; and the terms of their successors shall then begin.

Section 2. The Congress shall assemble at least once in every year, and such meeting shall begin at noon on the 3d day of January, unless they shall by law appoint a different day.

Adjusting the Timing

Think of this as a bridge between the Progressive amendments *and* the first flexing of New Deal Democratic muscles. Most of its provisions were first proposed in 1923 at the tail end of the Progressive Era, but it was only passed under the New Deal Democratic Congress of 1932. It fixed timing issues traceable to the slower world of 18th century travel and regarding passage of the Constitution.

Issues

The new United States government began work on March 4, 1789, a date chosen because it gave enough time after ratification for the complex electoral system to work and gave newly elected officials time to make their way to the nation's capital. (The Constitution was ratified as of June 21, 1788.)

Thus, Presidents and Congressmen stayed in power for four months after an election that they may have lost. Note, too that the Constitution mandated only one Congressional term per year, in December, a full 13 months after the election of a new Congress! Though with the support of majorities of both houses and the President's signature, they could and sometimes did meet earlier and more often, they generally met only during the Constitutionally-mandated periods. (See 1.4.2 above.)

January 3

The new Congress takes office on this day and begins its first session.

January 20

The new President and Vice President are sworn into power on this day at noon.

Section 3 Presidential Succession

If, at the time fixed for the beginning of the term of the President, the President elect shall have died, the Vice President elect shall become President. If a President shall not have been chosen before the time fixed for the beginning of his term, or if the President elect shall have failed to qualify, then the Vice President elect shall act as President until a President shall have qualified; and the Congress may by law provide for the case wherein neither a President elect nor a Vice President elect shall have qualified, declaring who shall then act as President, or the manner in which one who is to act shall be selected, and such person shall act accordingly until a President or Vice President shall have qualified.

Section 4. The Congress may by law provide for the case of the death of any of the persons from whom the House of Representatives may choose a President whenever the right of choice shall have devolved upon them, and for the case of the death of any of the persons from whom the Senate may choose a Vice President whenever the right of choice shall have devolved upon them.

Section 5. Sections 1 and 2 shall take effect on the 15th day of October following the ratification of this article.

Section 6. This article shall be inoperative unless it shall have been ratified as an amendment to the Constitution by the legislatures of three-fourths of the several States within seven years from the date of its submission.

Death of President or Vice President Elect

This section starts out simple and gets complicated. Simple: If the President elect dies between the time he or she is elected and noon on January 3 the Vice President elect is automatically to take his or her place as President.

Slightly less-simple: If there is a problem with the electoral status of the President elect then the Vice President-elect shall act as President until it is resolved.

Complicated: What happens if neither a President nor Vice President shall have been elected by January 20? Congress shall pass a law naming an acting president until a new President and Vice President can be elected. Fortunately, this last provision has never been put to the test. It imagines a situation where the new Congress is sworn in on January 3 and has to rule on who should become President as of noon on January 20, a law that would have to be passed by both houses and signed by the out-going President.

21st Amendment—Liquor Legalized

Proposed February 20, 1933. Ratified December 5, 1933.

Section 1. The eighteenth article of amendment to the Constitution of the United States is hereby repealed.

Section 2. The transportation or importation into any State, Territory, or possession of the United States for delivery or use therein of intoxicating liquors, in violation of the laws thereof, is hereby prohibited.

Section 3. This article shall be inoperative unless it shall have been ratified as an amendment to the Constitution by conventions in the several States, as provided in the Constitution, within seven years from the date of the submission hereof to the States by the Congress.

Repealed

The 18th remains the only amendment to the Constitution to be repealed. Its repeal reflects a major shift in American population from South and West to cities, a shift made more radical by the long wait to reapportion House seats to reflect changes in the 1920 census. The House reflected the more rural population distribution of America's 1910 census until 1929. The census reapportioned 21 seats away from Southern and Western states in 1929.

Original Package Doctrine (Packy Run)

"The transportation or importation into any state..."

This section for the first time empowers states to forbid interstate commerce in liquor. Prior to the 18th Amendment, even so-called "dry" states found it difficult to prevent interstate commerce in liquor. Congressional control over interstate commerce is plenary, and states were forbidden from interfering with it. The original case, *Brown v. Maryland* (1827) ruled that goods imported from one state were not taxable by another until they had been taken out of their original packaging and/or sold. The ruling in *Leisy v. Hardin* (1890) stated that as long as liquor was shipped in its original package states could not tax or regulate it.

(This is the origin of the terms "Package" or "Packy" Store or "Packy Run" as it refers to a store selling alcohol.) Thus, while repealing nationwide Prohibition, the 21st Amendment provided an exception to the commerce clause (1.8.3) and the Import-Export clause (1.10.2) as regards alcohol. The Court has considered several times whether this second section of the amendment gave states any additional exemptions to the Commerce Clause. It does not.

Local Wineries

Recently, the Court has considered whether states have been taking advantage of this clause to protect local wine makers. In short, states that permit in-state wineries to sell directly to consumers through the mail must permit out-of-state wineries to do the same. *Granholm v. Heald* (2005).

22nd Amendment— Two Terms for President

Proposed March 24, 1947. Ratified February 27, 1951.

Section 1. No person shall be elected to the office of the President more than twice, and no person who has held the office of President, or acted as President, for more than two years of a term to which some other person was elected President shall be elected to the office of the President more than once. But this Article shall not apply to any person holding the office of President when this Article was proposed by the Congress, and shall not prevent any person who may be holding the office of President, or acting as President, during the term within which this Article becomes operative from holding the office of President or acting as President during the remainder of such term.

Section 2. This article shall be inoperative unless it shall have been ratified as an amendment to the Constitution by the legislatures of three fourths of the several States within seven years from the date of its submission to the States by the Congress.

Term Limits on the President

This forces Presidents to adhere to George Washington's rule. Washington remains unusual among revolutionary leaders in world history for voluntarily relinquishing power. He resigned after the Revolutionary War, and after a second term as President announced that he would not run again. This decision came in part from his wish to go home, and to his age. It also came from a desire to embody the republican virtuousness that put public good ahead of private interest. He wished the office to outlive him.

Every president since Washington adhered to this tradition until Franklin D. Roosevelt. FDR's cousin Teddy Roosevelt had also chafed under it.

23rd Amendment—
Electoral Votes for Washington, DC

Proposed June 16, 1960. Ratified March 29, 1961.

Section 1. The District constituting the seat of Government of the United States shall appoint in such manner as the Congress may direct:

A number of electors of President and Vice President equal to the whole number of Senators and Representatives in Congress to which the District would be entitled if it were a State, but in no event more than the least populous State; they shall be in addition to those appointed by the States, but they shall be considered, for the purposes of the election of President and Vice President, to be electors appointed by a State; and they shall meet in the District and perform such duties as provided by the twelfth article of amendment.

Section 2. The Congress shall have power to enforce this article by appropriate legislation.

This amendment did no more than to grant residents of Washington, DC the right to vote in Presidential elections. It did *not* give Washington, DC any House or Senate representation.

24th Amendment—
Poll Taxes Prohibited

Proposed August 27, 1962. Ratified January 23, 1964.

Section 1. The right of citizens of the United States to vote in any primary or other election for President or Vice President, for electors for President or Vice President, or for Senator or Representative in Congress, shall not be denied or abridged by the United States or any State by reason of failure to pay any poll tax or other tax.

Section 2. The Congress shall have power to enforce this article by appropriate legislation.

Limited to Federal Elections Only

Note that this amendment only applied to federal elections. The Constitution largely leaves management of elections to the states.

Pay to Vote

The Court ruled that all citizens had the right to vote in all local elections as well, whether they had paid their taxes or not. *Harper v. Virginia Board of Electors* (1966).

25th Amendment— Presidential Succession

Proposed July 6, 1965. Ratified February 10, 1967.

Section 1. In case of the removal of the President from office or of his death or resignation, the Vice President shall become President.

Section 2. Whenever there is a vacancy in the office of the Vice President, the President shall nominate a Vice President who shall take office upon confirmation by a majority vote of both Houses of Congress.

Rules of Succession

The following presidents have died in office and been replaced by their Vice Presidents: William Henry Harrison (1841), Zachary Taylor (1850), Abraham Lincoln (1865), William McKinley (1901), Warren G. Harding (1923), Franklin D. Roosevelt (1945), John F. Kennedy (1963). In each case, the sitting Vice President rose to the Presidency, as laid out in the rule of succession in clause 2.1.6 above.

Selecting a New Vice President

Section 2 solved the problem of filling the office of Vice President between elections. Prior to this, when vacated for any reason, including promotion to President, the office of Vice President would remain vacant until the next election. The lack of a Vice President did not cripple the government, but it raised the issue of succession should the new President also become incapacitated or removed from office between elections.

25th Amendment, Cont'd

Section 3. Whenever the President transmits to the President pro tempore of the Senate and the Speaker of the House of Representatives his written declaration that he is unable to discharge the powers and duties of his office, and until he transmits to them a written declaration to the contrary, such powers and duties shall be discharged by the Vice President as Acting President.

Section 4. Whenever the Vice President and a majority of either the principal officers of the executive departments or of such other body as Congress may by law provide, transmit to the President pro tempore of the Senate and the Speaker of the House of Representatives their written declaration that the President is unable to discharge the powers and duties of his office, the Vice President shall immediately assume the powers and duties of the office as Acting President.

Thereafter, when the President transmits to the President pro tempore of the Senate and the Speaker of the House of Representatives his written declaration that no inability exists, he shall resume the powers and duties of his office unless the Vice President and a majority of either the principal officers of the executive department or of such other body as Congress may by law provide, transmit within four days to the President pro tempore of the Senate and the Speaker of the House of Representatives their written declaration that the President is unable to discharge the powers and duties of his office. Thereupon Congress shall decide the issue, assembling within forty-eight hours for that purpose if not in session. If the Congress, within twenty-one days after receipt of the latter written declaration, or, if Congress is not in session, within twenty-one days after Congress is required to assemble, determines by two-thirds vote of both Houses that the President is unable to discharge the powers and duties of his office, the Vice President shall continue to discharge the same as Acting President; otherwise, the President shall resume the powers and duties of his office.

Voluntary Incapacity

In case the President decides he or she cannot perform his or her duties for any reason, the Vice President becomes Acting President. The President so notifies the House and Senate of this decision, and it remains in force until the President rescinds it.

Involuntary Removal

But what if the President is so incapacitated as to be unable (or unwilling) to so notify House and Senate? In this case, a majority of the Cabinet makes this decision.

If removed involuntarily, the President may notify Congress that he or she is ready to resume office, essentially appealing this decision by a majority of the Cabinet. If the Vice President and Cabinet agree that the President is capable of serving, the President immediately resumes office. If they disagree, they have four days to so notify Congress, and Congress may agree with the Cabinet by 2/3 vote. If so, then the Vice President remains in office as Acting President. Otherwise, the President resumes office.

26th Amendment—
Eighteen-Year-Olds Gain the Vote

Proposed March 23, 1971. Ratified June 30, 1971.

Section 1. The right of citizens of the United States, who are eighteen years of age or older, to vote shall not be denied or abridged by the United States or by any State on account of age.

Section 2. The Congress shall have power to enforce this article by appropriate legislation.

Why Give 18-Year-Olds the Vote?

In his 1954 State of the Union speech, President Dwight D. Eisenhower devoted an entire section to suffrage. He recommended that Congress take action to grant the vote to the people of the District of Columbia, and that Hawaii be granted statehood. He asked that the states allow their overseas soldiers an easier way to vote. He also asked for a constitutional amendment allowing 18-year-old citizens to vote. He explicitly put this request in the context of 18-year-old citizens being called on to serve in the military. If they are to be asked to fight, he argued, they should have the right to participate politically in the decisions that cause them to risk their lives.

Federal Versus State Suffrage

In 1970, pressed by the unpopularity of the Vietnam War, Congress passed a law lowering the voting age for all elections at all levels. The 26th came as a response to the Court's narrow rule in *Oregon v. Mitchell* (1970) that Congress could not regulate state voting ages by law. See clause 1.2.1 above giving states the power to rule on the qualifications of Electors.

27th Amendment— Congressional Pay Raises Limited

Proposed September 25, 1789. Ratified May 7, 1992.

No law, varying the compensation for the services of the Senators and Representatives, shall take effect, until an election of Representatives shall have intervened.

This amendment fits nicely with the Emoluments clause, 1.6.2 that prevents lawmakers from holding additional jobs, or from leaving to take jobs that had been created or that had their pay raised since the lawmaker had been in office.

This amendment is an oddity in that it was proposed as one of the original Bill of Rights, but not ratified by a sufficient number of states. Since there was no explicit time limit on its passage, a college student who had researched the subject for a paper decided to campaign for its passage. He was more successful with his campaign than with the original paper, which received a "C" grade.

Beyond the Basics

The Constitution Ought to Be Simple

The Constitution ought to be simple. It consists of roughly 5,000 words. It's the length of a magazine article. It's written in plain English, not legalese. Nevertheless, once it went into effect, it got complicated.

From the start, Justices were pulled among at least four beasts at once: original meaning, accumulated precedent, modern need, and their private beliefs. Yet none of these was sufficient on its own.

Because the Framers themselves disagreed on much, whose original meaning should Justices look to for guidance? Much of the language was ambiguous. Nor can Justices of any era ignore new problems and popular politics of their world. Nor is any Justice free from human prejudices and prior beliefs. And to ignore existing precedent would be to undermine the present Court's authority and status.

Fortunately, this is a book of history, not prescription. The battle over what sort of interpretation *ought* to reign can be left to others. Whether or not interpretation of the Constitution *should* be based strictly on its original meaning, it hasn't been. History is an appropriate tool for understanding how the meaning of the Constitution has changed over time. The battle, after all, has been one of politics, power, and interest as much as judicial philosophy.

Indeed, the Constitution has bedeviled scholars and politicians (let alone students) from the very beginning. James Madison and Benjamin Franklin took opposite positions on Congress's right to address the issue of slavery in the Constitution's very first year of operation. Just a few years later, Alexander Hamilton and Thomas Jefferson adopted opposite positions on the meaning of the Necessary and Proper Clause. In 1803 Chief Justice John Marshall insisted that the Court had the right to rule on the

Constitutionality of actions taken by the other branches. But this explicit authority appears nowhere in the Constitution. And while his ruling has been accepted as a binding precedent since he made it, *he was forced to so insist.*

The Constitution has always existed within a body of theory. Thomas Jefferson sent James Madison crates of books to help prepare for the Convention in 1787. The Framers assumed a close knowledge of legal tradition, as well as *Blackstone's* and other legal guides.

The written US Constitution is part of an implicit set of constitutional ideas. It has never existed solely in itself. As John Marshall wrote in 1803, if it were all-inclusive, it would not be a Constitution; it would be a code of laws. "We should never forget," he wrote, "that it is a *Constitution* we are expounding."

The Constitution enshrined inherent conflicts within America's basic law, to be worked out in our politics. It included state *and* national powers; state *and* national citizenship; specific personal liberties *and* processes legitimated solely by their democratic nature. (The latter is a conflict because Americans can democratically decide to violate individual liberties, though the barriers are high.) At the same time, states vie with the national government; the Legislative, Executive, and Judicial branches vie with each other; different groups in society vie for power. In the midst of this raw battle for power, we insist that democratic processes be protected and that certain liberties remain sacred (or at least that they be protected by difficult-to-meet democratic standards). As Thomas Jefferson pointed out, the Constitution contained another inherent conflict: It attempted to impose the product of a single generation on all that followed.

Nevertheless, each generation of Americans has insisted that the Constitution also conform to our understanding of what is most valuable. America is a nation and a federation supposedly fallen from the innocence of our Revolutionary era. Since then we have at times fudged our democratic processes and violated our ideals of personal liberty. Yet as the wisest voices of the founding era knew, the fall was inevitable; a government of laws inevitably would become a government of people. A government of people would become one of powerful institutions and interests even as we sought to preserve our version of the ideals of our Revolution. Moreover, the Founders were no strangers to politics. Even the scholarly James Madison found that his election depended as much on the alcohol he provided voters on election day as on his virtues as a statesman.

The Constitutional crisis of slavery was another contradiction at the heart of our history: We found ourselves unable to defend at once the individual liberty of slaves as humans, *and* the property rights of slave owners, *and* state sovereignty. The Civil War (1861-1865) settled what we could not finesse in our politics or resolve in the decision-making processes of the Constitution. The victors of the Civil War forced the 13th, 14th, and 15th Amendments on the South. Ratification followed the Constitution's Article 5 processes, if imperfectly. Starting in the mid-1870s (a bare 10 years after the Civil War), America's political class decided to abandon the Civil War era Reconstruction amendments. Nevertheless, the 14th Amendment came back to the center of American constitutional-ism by the mid-20th century.

The Constitution remains a touchstone in the battle for American ideals of equality and self-limiting governance. Yet as Ben Franklin argued at the time, its success must be measured more in the actions of the people we elect, the laws we enact, and the ways that we enforce those laws rather than the text alone.

But more, the Constitution has become a way to explain a chang-ing sense of the United States as a nation. The definition of "the people" has changed since 1787, most radically through the Civil War and Reconstruction era from 1857-1876, and in the Liberal

Constitutionalism era that began in 1937 and arguably continues to this day.

The written Constitution is only a starting point for American constitutionalism. American constitutionalism is also a complex of accumulated traditions and understandings linked back to our origins as a people. (The 9th Amendment refers to additional, unwritten norms that exist and existed outside the Constitution itself.) It has been created and re-created in subsequent events such as Supreme Court decisions, elections, wars and crises, the rise of national-scale business, of Progressivism, The New Deal, and the Civil Rights Movement, and the Conservative Movement.

American Constitutionalism exists in the historical tension between the ideals of our national origins, historical memory, and current realities. It exists between the historic realities of our national origins and current ideals.

The Constitution was ambiguous, deliberately so. The founding generation did the best they could to create a document a majority of Americans in each state and region would accept. They could not simply assume a majority of states would ratify. They could not simply assume they were creating a single nation. Their audience was a fractious set of diverse semi-sovereign states.

Among other things, the Constitution had to be a sales brochure for itself. It avoided subjects that it had failed to fully resolve (slavery, judicial oversight, settled balance between state v. national power). It put a process of national and federal government formation in motion.

The Founders also created a governing document that restrained national governmental tyranny with a web of interlocking, checked and balanced democratic processes and institutions. At the same time they sought to name basic liberties that a national government must respect.

The Constitution was created to be willfully ambiguous. The Framers hoped it would clarify itself in action.

The Constitution acts as a constraint, not simply in the details of its provisions, but in the demand of America's political culture that we try to live up to our Revolutionary ideals. To this day, political groups fight to capture the flag of the founders. Who, they ask, best represents our founding ideals?

It is a complicated question because it really asks: Who best represents our founding ideals as we live them today? We make different assumptions about race and gender. The national government as well as the states now guarantees basic liberties (because of the transformative 14th Amendment). Today we have a stronger identity as a nation rather than as a collection of united states. We have a standing army, an internationally intertwined economy mostly made up of wage earners, and privately held corporations of a scale never anticipated by the Framers. The Framers assumed that most voters would be self-employed. They expected the wealthiest entities in society to be real people, not corporate people. They expected a politics without parties. (To name a few issues.)

Who best represents our founding ideals as refracted through our accumulated history? It is an argument worth having.

Acknowledgments

My efforts to teach about the Constitution have shaped my efforts to write about it. I could not have done this without the students who have engaged in this process with me. To my colleagues at Kutztown University of Pennsylvania, thank you for your insights and patience.

The inimitable Bashar Hanna first encouraged me to take this project seriously. He introduced me to Frank Burrows of Pearson/Penguin who has shepherded it to publication.

The Institute for Constitutional History sent me to a weeklong seminar at Yale Law School on the topic where I learned much, including the limits of my knowledge.

Patt McCloskey read the manuscript and pointed out innumerable errors and areas that I needed to fix. Thank you Patt for saving me from myself. My brother Tom made me take out most of the professor-speak. My parents Jane and Dan and sisters Liz and Kat wondered, usefully and often why it wasn't *done* yet.

In a book designed to fit in a pocket, errors of omission are inevitable. Please accept my apologies for leaving out your favorite key cases and issues.

Errors of commission are less inevitable, though some may be less errors, and more differences between my opinion and yours. I hope you will at least find that I have done partial justice, or at least minimal violence to the insights of those whose efforts preceded my own. Or at least that my work here represents an honest effort to get it right.

Sam and Sophia, you remind me of what History and Constitution are *for*. To the Wondrous Mrs. Arabel who makes all possible, thank you.

Bibliography

As with the rest of this book, please use the following brief bibliography as a starting point but do not be limited by it. Here's a useful scholarly cheat: If you find anything that interests you in these sources, check their footnotes and bibliographies, and use them to pursue your interests further. It's called "mining the footnotes" and it's a good habit to get into.

Reference Sources:

Max Farrand, *The Records of the Federal Convention of 1787*. This four-volume documentary history is invaluable for those who truly wish to investigate the Constitutional Convention itself and the thinking of the Framers at the time. It includes most known notes and other materials from and about the Convention. It's available in electronic form online, but is far more interesting to dip into in bound form. Use the 1987 edition (out of print, alas) for index, bibliography and additional material in Volume 4.

Federalist Papers (available in different editions and online). Articles published anonymously by Alexander Hamilton, James Madison, and John Jay to support ratification.

Anti-Federalist Papers Less-well-known essays opposing ratification of the Constitution.

www.findlaw.com. This is a reference site on American law.

www.supremecourtus.gov. This is the official site of the US Supreme Court. From here you can download recent opinions and gather additional information.

www.avalon.law.yale.edu. The Avalon Project is an amazing collection of legal documents going back to the beginning of recorded human history. Publicly available.

www.consource.org. The Consource project contains documents and sources on the Constitution.

www.jstor.org. This is a paid site that gives full-text access to thousands of scholarly journal articles. If you are at a college or university you should already have access.

LexisNexis. A terrific if expensive resource for up-to-date access to court rulings and news.

Sue Davis, ed. *Corwin and Peltason's Understanding the Constitution* (17th Edition) Wadsworth Publishing (2007). Still the most afford-able complete reference.

Leonard Levy, Kenneth L. Karst, Dennis J. Mahoney, eds. *Encyclopedia of the American Constitution* (4 vols.) Macmillan Publishing Co. (1990) (Available used only.)

Constitutional Law Casebooks are used to teach the Constitution to law students. There are many available new and used. These are particularly useful for giving you a sense of how lawyers think.

Books on the Constitution

The following are accessible books for non-specialists. Nevertheless, they require the reader to know the basics and to think abstractly about the subject. This list is incomplete. Hopefully these books will lead you to others on the subject.

Akhil Reed Amar,

> *America's Constitution: A Biography* (Random House Trade Paperbacks, 2006)
>
> *Bill of Rights: Creation and Reconstruction* (Yale University Press, 2000)

Terry Bouton, *Taming Democracy: The People, the Founders, and the Troubled Ending of the American Revolution* (Oxford, 2007)

Catherine Drinker Bowen, *Miracle at Philadelphia: The Story of the Constitutional Convention*, (Back Bay, 1986)

Michael Kent Curtis, *No State Shall Abridge: The Fourteenth Amendment and the Bill of Rights* (Duke, 1990)

Joseph Ellis, *Founding Brothers: The Revolutionary Generation* (Vintage, 2002) (Alfred A. Knopf, 2000)

Don E. Fehrenbacher, *Slavery, Law, and Politics: The Dred Scott Case in Historical Perspective* (Oxford, 1981)

Barry Friedman, *The Will of the People: How Public Opinion Has Influenced the Supreme Court and Shaped the Meaning of the Constitution* (Farrar, Straus, 2009)

Jack P. Greene, *Peripheries and Center: Constitutional Development in the Extended Polities of the British Empire and the United States, 1607-1788* (Univ. Georgia, 1986)

Paul Kens, *Lochner v. New York: Economic Regulation on Trial* (University Press of Kansas, 1998)

Alex Keyssar, *The Right to Vote: The Contested History of Democracy in the United States* (Basic Books, Revised Edition, 2009) (Originally published, Basic Books 2000)

David E. Kyvig, *Explicit and Authentic Acts: Amending the U.S. Constitution, 1776-1995* (Univ. Press of Kansas, 1998)

Leonard W. Levy,

Origins of the Fifth Amendment: The Right Against Self-Incrimination (Ivan R. Dee, 1999) (Oxford, 1968)

Origins of the Bill of Rights (Yale, 2001)

Anthony Lewis, *Make No Law: The Sullivan Case and the First Amendment* (Vintage, 1992)

Jack N. Rakove, *Original Meanings: Politics and Ideas in the Making of the Constitution* (Vintage, 1997)

Michael A. Ross, *Justice of Shattered Dreams: Samuel Freeman Miller and the Supreme Court during the Civil War Era* (Louisiana State University Press, 2003)

Mark Tushnet, *A Court Divided: The Rehnquist Court and the Future of Constitutional Law* (W.W. Norton & Co. 2005)

Garry Wills, *Lincoln at Gettysburg: The Words That Remade America* (Simon & Schuster, 1992)

Gordon Wood, *Radicalism of the American Revolution* (Vintage, 1993)

Index